# Business English Meetings
## Instant Agendas

Jeremy Comfort and Nick Brieger

SERIES EDITOR: NICK BRIEGER

PENGUIN BOOKS

Published by the Penguin Group
Penguin Books Limited, 27 Wrights Lane, London W8 5TZ, England
Penguin Putnam Inc., 375 Hudson Street, New York, New York 10014, USA
Penguin Books Australia Limited, Ringwood, Victoria, Australia
Penguin Books Canada Limited, 10 Alcorn Avenue, Toronto, Ontario, Canada M4V 3B2
Penguin Books (NZ) Limited, Private Bag 102902, NSMC, Auckland, New Zealand

Penguin Books Limited, Registered Offices: Harmondsworth, Middlesex, England

Published by Penguin Books 1998
10 9 8 7 6 5 4 3 2

Copyright © Jeremy Comfort and Nick Brieger 1998
All rights reserved

The moral rights of the authors have been asserted

The publishers' make grateful acknowledgement to Barnaby's Picture Library for permission
to reprint the photographs on p.158.

Printed in England by William Clowes Limited, Beccles and London
Set in New Century Schoolbook and Helvetica

Except in the United States of America, this book is sold subject to the condition that it
shall not, by way of trade or otherwise, be lent, resold, hired out, or otherwise circulated
without the publishers' prior consent in any form of binding or cover other than that in
which it is published and without a similar condition including this condition being
imposed on the subsequent purchaser

**Photocopying notice**
The pages in the book marked From Business English Meetings by Jeremy Comfort and
Nick Brieger © Penguin Books 1998 **PHOTOCOPIABLE** may be photocopied free
of charge for classroom use by the purchasing individual or institution. This permission to
copy does not extend to branches or additional schools of an institution. All other copying
is subject to permission from the publisher.

# Contents

| | |
|---|---|
| Introduction | v |
| **Student's Notes** | 1 |
| **Teacher's Notes** | 3 |
| **Agendas** | 37 |

**Case study agendas**

| | | |
|---|---|---|
| 1 Company language | 38 |
| 2 Competition | 40 |
| 3 Corruption | 42 |
| 4 Dress | 44 |
| 5 The environment | 46 |
| 6 Equal opportunities | 48 |
| 7 Food terrorism | 50 |
| 8 Going international | 52 |
| 9 Information flow | 54 |
| 10 International assignments | 56 |
| 11 International joint venture | 58 |
| 12 Managing the project | 60 |
| 13 The millennium meeting | 62 |
| 14 Multicultural project | 64 |
| 15 New technology | 66 |
| 16 Outsourcing | 68 |
| 17 Pay versus benefits | 70 |
| 18 Quality | 72 |
| 19 Relocation | 74 |
| 20 Reorganization | 76 |
| 21 The safety committee | 78 |
| 22 Teleworking | 80 |
| 23 Training weekend | 82 |
| 24 Workload | 84 |

**Staff committee meetings**

| | |
|---|---|
| Staff committee meeting 1 | 87 |
| Staff committee meeting 2 | 88 |
| Staff committee meeting 3 | 90 |
| Staff committee meeting 4 | 92 |
| Staff committee meeting 5 | 94 |
| Staff committee meeting 6 | 96 |
| Staff committee meeting 7 | 98 |
| Staff committee meeting 8 | 100 |

**Specialist agendas**

| | |
|---|---|
| 1 Management | 102 |
| 2 Quality | 104 |
| 3 Human resources (1) | 106 |
| 4 Promotion | 108 |
| 5 The training dilemma | 110 |
| 6 Sales and marketing | 112 |
| 7 Finance | 114 |
| 8 Legal affairs | 116 |
| 9 Human resources (2) | 118 |
| 10 Production | 120 |

**Decision-making agendas**

| | |
|---|---|
| 1 Outsourcing or not? | 122 |
| 2 New training manager | 124 |
| 3 The budget | 126 |

**Problem-solving meetings**

| | |
|---|---|
| 1 Time management | 128 |
| 2 Staff morale | 130 |
| 3 Personality clash | 132 |
| 4 Working time and lunch-time | 134 |
| 5 Use of the Internet | 136 |
| 6 Poaching | 138 |
| 7 Delegation | 140 |
| 8 Open-plan | 142 |
| 9 Training course vs. on-the-job training | 144 |
| 10 Employment of disabled people | 146 |
| 11 Recycling | 148 |
| 12 An attractive remuneration package | 150 |

**Strategy meetings**

| | |
|---|---|
| 1 Mission statement | 152 |
| 2 Job advertisement | 154 |
| 3 Market research questionnaire | 156 |
| 4 Early retirement document | 158 |

**Brainstorming meetings**

| | |
|---|---|
| 1 Managing your time | 160 |
| 2 Management tools | 161 |
| 3 What's in a name? | 162 |
| 4 A new logo | 164 |
| 5 The company excursion | 166 |

**Language functions for meetings** 167

# Introduction

## To the teacher

**Business English Meetings** has been written in response to the demand for more materials to develop professional communication skills in the classroom. Its aim is to give foreign students of Business English specific practice in the skills and language of meetings in order to develop fluency and effectiveness. The material addresses a wide range of adult themes from a variety of professional areas, however, most of the activities do not require specialist knowledge. The material is completely independent of any course book and can, therefore, be used on any Business English course.

**Business English Meetings** consists of sixty-six activities. The activities are in one book containing:

- the details of the agenda for each meeting
- the role information for the students
- teacher's notes
- handling notes for meetings
- language notes for meetings.

## Target learners

The activities are aimed at learners of Business English at intermediate level or above. All the activities can be done by in-service learners: people who need English for their work. Most of the activities can also be done in their existing form by pre-service learners: people training for a career in the business world. The few remaining activities can be done by pre-service learners after minor adaptations have been made and explanations of key concepts have been given by the teacher.

## Description and organization

The book contains sixty-six meeting activities. These are arranged in sections, according to the type of meeting (*see* Contents page). The activities can be done in any order. All the information for each activity is given in the book, though students should be encouraged to contribute their own ideas and professional experience to the role-plays. Each activity consists of:

- an agenda or background brief to the meeting
- the student roles, where necessary.

All of the activities are intended for groups. In some cases the number of participants has been specified by the roles allocated, in others, the number of participants is open. Where specific roles have been allocated; the teacher can add or reduce the number of participants by making small changes to the agenda.

*Introduction*

## Activity types

The agendas are divided into seven sections; each contains agendas for different types of meetings:

1. Case studies (24 agendas)
2. Staff committee meetings (8 agendas)
3. Specialist meetings (10 agendas)
4. Decision-making meetings (3 agendas)
5. Problem-solving meetings (12 agendas)
6. Strategy meetings (4 agendas)
7. Brainstorming meetings (5 agendas).

The aim is to provide a wide range of contexts and meeting types. For more information about the meeting types *see* pp. 15–19.

## Communication skills

By doing the activities, students will practise communication skills and develop effective communication techniques. Thus they focus on both fluency and effectiveness.

## Timing

Effective meetings require careful preparation by all participants. Therefore, *before the meeting itself*, it is important for the teacher to brief the students on:

- their roles
- the procedures for the meeting
- the timing for the meeting
- the training objectives of the activity.

Most of the meetings will take at least an hour to complete; in addition, the teacher will need to set aside time for giving feedback on the various elements that make up effective meetings. (*See* Teacher's notes.)

## Additional resources

As some of the activities involve figures, a pocket calculator may be useful.

## To the teacher: Effective meetings template

The key to improving performance is to agree first what constitutes an effective meeting. The following model, though not exhaustive, captures many points which are relevant to different types of meetings and provides a useful template for performance feedback and evaluation.

**People** refers to everyone involved in the meeting and their roles:

- the chairperson/the participants/the secretary
- the boss/the subordinate
- the expert/the non-expert

Are the right people present in order to achieve the purpose of the meeting? Do they know what roles they are expected to fulfil?

*Introduction*

**Procedures** refers to the steps and stages of the meeting and their management. The style of meetings can vary enormously: from informal to formal; from highly controlled to very free; from impersonal to personal. Whatever the style, all meetings will benefit from some supportive chairing. It is the chairperson who can ensure that the meeting achieves its objectives.

The *chairperson* is responsible for overall control, in particular:

1 opening the meeting by introducing:
   a) the objectives
   b) the agenda
   c) the participants (if necessary)
   d) the procedure (order of speaking etc.)
   e) the timing
   f) the output (minutes, report, etc.).
2 facilitating and moderating by:
   a) making sure everybody gets a chance to speak
   b) interrupting speakers who talk too much
   c) encouraging speakers who talk too little.
3 summarizing by making sure everybody knows what has been said/agreed.
4 controlling the procedures by:
   a) keeping an eye on the time
   b) handling the agenda, for example, by cutting an item or shortening discussion.
5 concluding the meeting by:
   a) closing the meeting
   b) making sure the action/decisions are clear to everybody.

The roles of the *participants* are more open-ended. However, they can be summarized as:

1 contributing through a mini-presentation.
   In this case, the **participant** presents a point. Make sure it is clearly presented and is concise. (KISS: Keep it short and simple)
2 contributing through discussion, involving:
   a) giving and seeking opinions
   b) interrupting
   c) commenting
   d) agreeing and disagreeing
   e) advising and suggesting
   f) requesting information and action
   g) checking and confirming information.

The **secretary** is responsible for recording:
   a) the names of the participants
   b) the topics discussed
   c) brief details of arguments for and against
   d) decisions made
   e) voting details
   f) follow-up actions to be carried out (who, what and when)
   g) the date, time and place of the next meeting
   h) distributing the minutes within a reasonable time.

*Introduction*

**Results** refers to the outcomes of the meeting. A lot of meetings fail because the participants are unsure of the purpose and therefore dissatisfied with the results. Therefore effective meetings depend entirely on:

- communicating the purpose
- satisfying expectations
- clarifying the outcome in terms of action.

**Language** refers to the traditional categories of language forms:

- grammar
- **Key vocabulary**
- pronunciation.

Are these used correctly?

In order to derive the greatest benefit from classroom time on short courses, it is important that classroom activities focus on meeting practice and feedback. This means that once the elements of effective meetings have been agreed, classroom activities move through a series of preparatory steps to the meeting itself – the practice through which the learners aim to improve their performance in an observable way in one or more of the above areas.

So, referring to the effective meetings template, the main concerns of typical Business English learners can be summarized as:

- the procedural elements
- the linguistic elements
- practice
- feedback.

## Using the material

Instant agendas provides the teacher with great flexibility in organizing simulated and role-play meetings.

Whichever agenda you choose, a successful meeting will depend on the following factors:

1 Understanding the situation and roles: students must be given time to grasp what the meeting is about and their role.

2 Appointing a chairperson: all of the meetings will benefit from someone to lead the meeting; this role can be rotated within the meeting (from item to item) to give other students a chance to chair.

3 Setting clear objectives in terms of:
   a) output of the meeting ( a decision, recommendation, etc.)
   b) communication skills (chairing, participating, etc.)
   c) language knowledge (functions, vocabulary, grammar).

## Stages of the activity – standard procedures

*Before the meeting*

1 Choose an agenda.
   The agendas are all concerned with issues from the business world. Some, however, are more specialist than others. Choose an agenda which suits the interests and/or knowledge of your group.

*Introduction*

The sixty-six agendas are arranged in seven sections:

*Section 1     Case study agendas (1–24)*
These are based around a situation. Roles are described in terms of position in the company and position on the agenda items.

*Section 2     Staff committee meetings (1–8)*
These are composed of six different situations. Participants have no specific role. The objective is to make recommendations to the Board.

*Section 3     Specialist agendas (1–10)*
These agendas focus around issues concerning a single management area or the problems faced by one department. Therefore they lend themselves to working with groups of students who work in or are studying the same function (e.g. marketing, finance, etc.).

*Section 4     Decision-making agendas (1–3)*
These agendas present more complex situations. Roles are allocated and difficult decisions have to be taken.

*Section 5     Problem-solving meetings (1–12)*
These agendas require creative, problem-solving skills. Roles are kept to a minimum.

*Section 6     Strategy meetings (1–4)*
These agendas are based around strategic business issues often involving a written document after the meeting decisions have been taken. Roles are kept to a minimum.

*Section 7     Brainstorming meetings (1–5)*
These are creative meetings in which an idea/name/design has to be created. The roles are fairly minimal, allowing students to express their own ideas to a large extent. This type of meeting typically has no agenda. However, it still requires a framework and some control to be successful.

2  Assign roles.
The chairman (or chairperson) has overall control of the meeting. In some agendas, the role of chairperson is fixed; in others either you or the participants can choose who will chair the meeting. There are different styles of chairing. Some people have a more autocratic manner and control the meeting more strictly; others have a more organic manner and let the meeting flow. You should give different students the possibility to chair meetings. This is important for three reasons:

- it allows them to gain confidence in that role
- they get feedback on their performance from the other participants and the teacher
- it helps them develop their skills.

3  Give time for preparation.
Every meeting needs preparation. The handling notes for each agenda suggest the length of time for preparation. This is only a guideline. Some groups may need more time, others less. The preparation can be done either in class or, where possible, at home. It is also important to tell the students what to prepare. This will vary with each agenda. However, as each meeting is intended to provide free practice, participants should not come with notes to be read to the meeting. Rather, they should have prepared notes of what they intend to say. The chairperson may need to refer, during the meeting, to the language for chairing a meeting (*see* pages 167-69).

4  Make sure they know your objectives in terms of language and communication.
These practice meetings are intended to provide material for developing:

- accuracy of language knowledge
- fluency of general communication
- effectiveness of professional communication.

*Introduction*

Accuracy reflects the correct use of language forms; fluency the smooth flow of language; and effectiveness the ability to use appropriate behaviour and procedures in order to have the right impact on the other members of the meeting. It is important for you to clarify what the focus of the activity is. In this way, the students will focus on the content of the meeting, but also on aspects of their performance.

*During the meeting*

1. Take notes on language and communication strengths and weaknesses.
    In order to provide feedback after the meeting, you will need to agree objectives before the meeting (*see* 4 above). During the meeting you should make notes on those elements of language or communication that will provide the basis for feedback to individuals and/or to the group. Remember that learners respond to both positive and negative feedback. Therefore, you should aim to strike a balance between what was wrong and what was right (language), what was good and what was not so good (communication).
2. Use a video or audio cassette recorder to give you a record of their performance.
    Recording the meeting can be a useful way of providing feedback. However, it can also be time-consuming and ineffective to watch a whole meeting again. It is, perhaps, useful to record, where possible, and then watch/listen to selected passages which illustrate good practice and/or poor practice.
3. Try to be a 'fly on the wall'. Do not intrude in the meeting.
    Your presence should be as a silent supporter, providing help where absolutely necessary. Help might be needed if a participant is stuck for a word, or the group is stuck for a strategy.

*After the meeting*

1. Ask the students what they thought of the meeting.
    As meetings are a group activity, the participants should be invited to share their experience with you and with the others. Of course, you will be the arbiter of language, but they should be encouraged to provide feedback on fluency and effectiveness – their own and others'.
2. Give the students coherent feedback on communication skills (chairing, participating etc.).
    To be effective, the teacher's feedback on communication skills should be based on a framework; such as 'Procedures for the chairperson' on page 1.
3. Give them more detailed feedback on language use.
    You will need to be selective as to how much language feedback to give. It is important to remember to balance positive and negative feedback, to tell the group what language was good and what was not so good.

# How to . . .

1. Choose a chairman and appoint a secretary.
    Every meeting needs a chairman and a secretary. Everyone should have a chance to undertake both roles. Therefore, either you can choose or the group can choose. If you plan to have a series of meetings, the role(s) could be rotated on a fixed basis so that each person knows when they will have a chance to chair, participate and write minutes.
2. Reach a decision.
    An effective meeting needs a result. In these practice materials, this will be a decision. The decision may be unanimous, but it needn't be. In general, to be effective, any decision needs to reached according to agreed procedures (technically correct) and accepted by the majority of the group (attitudinally appropriate). The precise mechanism for reaching a decision will depend on the local meeting culture. In some cases voting may be appropriate; in others the participants will express their decision to the rest of the group.
3. Write an output document.
    The materials suggest documents that are to be produced after the meeting, including minutes,

# Introduction

memos and action plans. In addition, the strategy meetings integrate writing documents within the aims of the meeting.

*Minutes*

Minutes are an official record of the decision of the meeting. They should include:

- the names of the members attending
- the topics discussed
- concise details of arguments for and against
- motions carried and rejected
- voting details, where appropriate
- responsibility for actions agreed by the meeting.

*Memos*

Memos (memoranda) provide a brief report or instructions. There is no precise format for memos. It will depend on the audience and the purpose. Headings can include:

- the person(s) to whom the memo is addressed
- all who are to be made aware of its contents
- the name of the sender
- the date
- the subject matter.

*Action plan*

Action plans take the decisions of a meeting and formalize them so that there is a clear framework for carrying the action through. There is no precise format for action plans. However, they should include:

- who (the name(s) of the person(s) who are to carry out the action)
- what (the action)
- when (the timescale or deadline).

They may also include:

- how (the methods or tools to be used)
- where (the place for the action(s) to be carried out).

*Other documents*

The above list should not limit the output documents to be produced and you should feel free to agree or set other writing tasks.

# Student's notes

## Planning and preparing for a meeting

These agendas will give you practice in two main skills:

1 Chairing meetings
2 Participating in meetings.

You will find notes on the procedures on pages 1–2 and notes on language to support these procedures on page 167 ff. Having selected an agenda, it will help if you follow these steps:

*Before the meeting*
1 Study the agenda/situation; make sure you understand the objectives.
2 Prepare your role (sometimes you will be expected to present a point; other times respond to other people).
3 Note key language (vocabulary and expressions) which you feel will be useful during the meeting.

*During the meeting*
1 Listen actively (clarify when necessary, show agreement where appropriate).
2 Take your opportunity to speak (interrupt and get your point across).
3 Speak clearly; check everybody understands your point.

*After the meeting*
1 Give your teacher feedback on what you thought of the meeting.
2 Reflect on your communication skills (chairing, participating).
3 Reflect on your language use.

*Special notes on chairing*
Sometimes you will be allocated the role of the chairperson. Study the chairing notes below.

## The procedures of meetings

The following list shows the major moves that are required for:

- the chairperson
- the participants
- the secretary.

Some steps are fairly mechanical and ritualized, e.g. opening the meeting and thanking participants for their participation; others, such as summarizing the various views around the table are more complex (conceptually and linguistically); and yet others may be more dependent on the meeting type or the agreed conventions. So, you should view the procedures as a starting point for exploring different styles rather than as a list of rules to be followed.

*Procedures for the chairperson*

- Open the meeting.
- State purpose/objectives of meeting.
- Welcome new participants, if necessary.
- Give apologies for absence.
- Read secretary's report of last meeting.
- Deal with Matters Arising from report.
- Introduce agenda for current meeting and review/amend/prioritize, as necessary.

## Student's notes

- Introduce item 1 and invite oral report.
- Invite discussion, if appropriate.
- Summarize points discussed.
- Lead into decision-making process, if appropriate.
- Conclude point and thank presenter.
- Introduce next item and invite report, until all points have been covered or time has run out.
- Summarize points covered and decisions made. Relate to objectives.
- Invite Any Other Business (AOB).
- Agree time, date and place for next meeting.
- Thank participants for attending.
- Close meeting.

*Procedures for the participants*

- Present information in the form of an oral report or mini-presentation
- Participate in discussion, involving:
  giving and seeking opinions
    – interrupting
    – commenting
    – agreeing and disagreeing
    – advising and suggesting
    – requesting information and action
    – checking and confirming information.

*Procedures for the secretary.*

To record:

- the names of the participants
- the topics discussed
- brief details of arguments for and against
- decisions made
- voting details
- follow-up actions to be carried out (who, what and when)
- the date, time and place of the next meeting.

**Note:** The list of phrases in 'Language functions for meetings' (*see* pp. 167–69) shows the language corresponding to the steps to be carried out.

# Teacher's notes

## Case study 1
### *Company language*

*Introduction*

This case deals with the role of English as the language of international communication. This can be a sensitive and controversial issue where it is felt that English is undermining the local language(s) and culture. However, English usage and the interest in English language learning are both growing at a dramatic rate. The figure of 1.2 billion users of English (estimated 1997) is set to rise as more and more non-native speakers use the language as a tool of international communication.

The six roles provide a forum in which different views about the international role of English and its impact on the local environment can be explored.

*Lead-in*

Warm up the group by discussing:
- the current role of English in local companies
- the future role of English in an international environment
- the benefits of having a single international language
- the risks of having a single international language.

*Method*

(*See also* 'Stages of the activity – standard procedures', p. viii.)

1. After the lead-in discussion, look at the case itself.
2. Ask your students to read through the issue.
3. Make sure they all fully understand the case.
4. Assign roles (not only functional roles, but also a secretary to take minutes).
5. Allow 5 minutes to read through, prepare roles and language (*see* pp. viii–ix).
6. Agree on the timing for the meeting.
7. Run the meeting (audio- or video-record it if possible).
8. Give the students language and communication feedback.

*Follow-up*

(*See also* 'How to . . . write an output document', p. x.)

- This type of case lends itself to written follow-up in the form of:

    i) a memo about training policy to be circulated throughout the company

    ii) a document drawn up by the training department explaining their role in supporting (or not supporting) English training.

- Encourage your students to draw up check-lists for improved performance in their next meeting.

*Key vocabulary*

communication skills – language skills
domination
growing influence
language training
local culture

*Teacher's notes*

## Case study 2

### Competition

*Introduction*
This case deals with contracts of employment and, in particular, competition clauses which attempt to prevent employees from leaving the company and taking customers with them. This is always a difficult legal issue as, however tight the legal contract, the courts will often favour the individual over the organization, arguing that you cannot stop someone from trying to earn a living.

None of the six roles require special expertise, although it is usually best to assign roles according to professional interest.

*Lead-in*
Warm up the group by discussing the issue of competition. Do your students feel all forms of competition should be allowed? Or should the authorities try to protect people from the worst effects of competition?

*Method*
(*See also* 'Stages of the activity – standard procedures', p. viii.)
1 After the lead-in discussion, look at the case itself.
2 Ask your students to read through the issue.
3 Make sure they all fully understand the case.
4 Assign roles (not only functional roles, but also a secretary to take minutes).
5 Allow 5 minutes to read through, prepare roles and language (*see* pp. viii–ix).
6 Agree on the timing for the meeting.
7 Run the meeting (audio- or video-record it if possible).
8 Give the students language and communication feedback.

*Follow-up*
(*See also* 'How to . . . write an output document', p. x.)
- This type of case lends itself to written follow-up in the form of minutes or a memo.
- Encourage your students to draw up check-lists for improved performance in their next meeting.

*Key vocabulary*
clause in a contract
contract – to break a contract
law – legal – to break the law
to compete – competition
to resign – to hand in your resignation
to take to court
to tighten a contract

## Case study 3

### Corruption

*Introduction*
This case deals with the issue of corruption in business. Discussion will be focused on the fine line between looking after your customers and actually bribing them. There are large differences in what is interpreted as corruption in different business cultures. Teachers should be aware of what is considered as corruption in the culture they are working in.

*Lead-in*
Discuss the meaning of the word corruption. What do your students consider as corrupt in business and other walks of life? This discussion could be widened to talk about ethics in business and what is considered as ethical/unethical.

*Method*
(*See also* 'Stages of the activity – standard procedures', p. viii.)
1 After the lead-in discussion, look at the case itself.
2 Ask your students to read through the issue.
3 Make sure they all fully understand the case.
4 Assign roles (not only functional roles, but also a secretary to take minutes).
5 Allow 5 minutes to read through, prepare roles and language (*see* pp. viii–ix).
6 Agree on the timing for the meeting.
7 Run the meeting (audio- or video-record it if possible).
8 Give the students language and communication feedback.

*Follow-up*
(*See also* 'How to . . . write an output document', p. x.)
Different written follow-up tasks can be set:
- a memo informing staff of new guidelines
- minutes of the meeting (including actions)
- draft regulations.

*Key vocabulary*
bribe – to bribe – bribery
company/corporate image
corrupt – corruption
libel – to sue for libel
to abuse – abuse
to be in the headlines
to take to court
to win a case
'wining and dining'

Teacher's notes

## Case study 4

### Dress

**Introduction**

Dress code in a company is usually a reflection of the culture of the organization. However, some people in the front line with customers may feel they have to dress formally whatever the internal culture of the company. This case focuses on the potential conflict in this area.

**Lead-in**

Discuss with the students what sort of dress is appropriate in their working cultures. Are there differences between the dress code of those dealing with customers and those only working internally? What are the dress codes for men and women?

**Method**

(*See also* 'Stages of the activity – standard procedures', p. viii.)

1 After the lead-in discussion, look at the case itself.
2 Ask your students to read through the issue.
3 Make sure they all fully understand the case.
4 Assign roles (not only functional roles, but also a secretary to take minutes).
5 Allow 5 minutes to read through, prepare roles and language (*see* pp. viii–ix).
6 Agree on the timing for the meeting.
7 Run the meeting (audio- or video-record it if possible).
8 Give the students language and communication feedback.

**Follow-up**

(*See also* 'How to . . . write an output document', p. x.)

- Written minutes or a memo spelling out the dress code of the company could be written.
- A survey on dress codes amongst your participants/institution could be another lively follow-up task.

**Key vocabulary**

dress
shirt
skirt
suit
T-shirt
tie
casual clothes
formal clothes
jeans
scruffily dressed
smartly dressed

## Case study 5

### Environment

**Introduction**

This case centres round the clash between environmental and financial constraints. Many businesses have to resolve similar conflicts of interest. There is no legal issue involved here, it is simply a matter of balancing opposing interests.

**Lead-in**

Find out where your students stand on environmental issues. What sort of laws are enforced to protect the environment? How important is a good working environment – is it a priority?

**Method**

(*See also* 'Stages of the activity – standard procedures', p. viii.)

1 After the lead-in discussion, look at the case itself.
2 Ask your students to read through the issue.
3 Make sure they all fully understand the case.
4 Assign roles (not only functional roles, but also a secretary to take minutes).
5 Allow 5 minutes to read through, prepare roles and language (*see* pp. viii–ix).
6 Agree on the timing for the meeting.
7 Run the meeting (audio- or video-record it if possible).
8 Give the students language and communication feedback.

**Follow-up**

(*See also* 'How to . . . write an output document', p. x.)
The output from the meeting could be:

- a written memo to all staff
- a brief presentation to staff.

**Key vocabulary**

purpose-built office block
site
split-site
extension
relocation
space
to stock (with fish)
wildlife habitat

*Teacher's notes*

## Case study 6

### *Equal opportunities*

*Introduction*

This case deals with equal job opportunities for men and women in a traditionally male environment: coal mining. It provides an opportunity for discussing whether there are:

- jobs for which one sex is better suited
- work environments for which one sex is better suited.

*Lead-in*

Warm up the group by discussing:

- if there is equality of opportunity in their local working environment(s)
- if job equality is desirable
- what steps should be taken to improve the working environment for men and women.

*Method*

(*See also* 'Stages of the activity – standard procedures', p. viii.)

1. After the lead-in discussion, look at the case itself.
2. Ask your students to read through the issue.
3. Make sure they all fully understand the case.
4. Assign roles (not only functional roles, but also a secretary to take minutes).
5. Allow 5 minutes to read through, prepare roles and language (*see* pp. viii–ix).
6. Agree on the timing for the meeting.
7. Run the meeting (audio- or video-record it if possible).
8. Give the students language and communication feedback.

*Follow-up*

(*See also* 'How to . . . write an output document', p. x.)

- This type of case lends itself to written follow-up in the form of a policy document on the employment of women at BritPit.
- Encourage your students to draw up check-lists for improved performance in their next meeting.

*Key vocabulary*

human error
jobsharing
legislation
man's world – a male preserve – male-dominated
physical strength
productivity
profitable – profitability
sceptical

## Case study 7

### *Food terrorism*

*Introduction*

This case focuses on the ability of lobby groups to hit soft targets in their efforts to change society. Activists, aiming to protect animals, may have sabotaged food products in a supermarket in order to raise awareness of their campaign. At first sight, the resulting publicity could damage the supermarket's reputation. On the other hand, all publicity can be seen as good publicity.

*Lead-in*

Warm up the group by discussing:

- which lobby groups are active in their society
- what methods they use to raise awareness
- the effects of their actions
- whether their methods are justified
- what they achieve

*Method*

(*See also* 'Stages of the activity – standard procedures', p. viii.)

1. After the lead-in discussion, look at the case itself.
2. Ask your students to read through the issue.
3. Make sure they all fully understand the case.
4. Assign roles (not only functional roles, but also a secretary to take minutes).
5. Allow 5 minutes to read through, prepare roles and language (*see* pp. viii–ix).
6. Agree on the timing for the meeting.
7. Run the meeting (audio- or video-record it if possible).
8. Give the students language and communication feedback.

*Follow-up*

(*See also* 'How to . . . write an output document', p. x.)

- This case lends itself to written follow-up in the form of:

    i) an action plan for the parties involved
    ii) a statement to the press.

- Encourage your students to draw up check-lists for improved performance in their next meeting.

*Key vocabulary*

activist – animal activist
false alarm
hoax
hostile
scare
to contaminate
to withdraw

*Teacher's notes*

# Case study 8

## *Going international*

### *Introduction*
This case deals with internationalization. It raises questions of:
- the desirability of doing business across national borders
- the methodology for international operations
- the opportunities and threats of internationalization.

### *Lead-in*
Warm up the group by discussing:
- which local companies work in an international environment
- what opportunities they see of internationalization
- what threats they see of internationalization.

### *Method*
(*See also* 'Stages of the activity – standard procedures', p. viii.)
1. After the lead-in discussion, look at the case itself.
2. Ask your students to read through the issue.
3. Make sure they all fully understand the case.
4. Assign roles (not only functional roles, but also a secretary to take minutes).
5. Allow 5 minutes to read through, prepare roles and language (*see* pp. viii–ix).
6. Agree on the timing for the meeting.
7. Run the meeting (audio- or video-record it if possible).
8. Give the students language and communication feedback.

### *Follow-up*
(*See also* 'How to . . . write an output document', p. x.)
- This case lends itself to written follow-up in the form of:
  i) a statement formalizing the partners' position on internationalization
  ii) an action plan of any steps to be taken to implement the policy.
- Encourage your students to draw up check-lists for improved performance in their next meeting.

### *Key vocabulary*
costs – to reduce costs
job opportunities
productivity – to increase productivity
to downsize
to expand
to rationalize
xenophobia – xenophobic

# Case study 9

## *Information flow*

### *Introduction*
This case deals with sharing communication and how to get the right balance in terms of quantity and quality. Meetings are the main forum for exchanging information. However, many managers complain that they spend too much time in meetings. The question for the meeting is how to balance the need for communication in a busy company.

### *Lead-in*
Warm up the group by discussing:
- how much time they spend in meetings
- if meetings provide the best forum for exchanging opinions
- if their meetings could be improved.

### *Method*
(*See also* 'Stages of the activity – standard procedures', p. viii.)
1. After the lead-in discussion, look at the case itself.
2. Ask your students to read through the issue.
3. Make sure they all fully understand the case.
4. Assign roles (not only functional roles, but also a secretary to take minutes).
5. Allow 5 minutes to read through, prepare roles and language (*see* pp. viii–ix).
6. Agree on the timing for the meeting.
7. Run the meeting (audio- or video-record it if possible).
8. Give the students language and communication feedback.

### *Follow-up*
(*See also* 'How to . . . write an output document', p. x.)
- This case lends itself to written follow-up in the form of guidelines for meetings.

### *Key vocabulary*
chairperson – to appoint a chairperson
communication
meetings (discussion, decision-making, briefing, brainstorming)
minutes – to write the minutes – to circulate the minutes
time-keeping
to run a meeting
to streamline
to transmit messages

*Teacher's notes*

## Case study 10

### *International assignments*

*Introduction*
This case centres around the role and work of 'international' managers. Many companies face the problem of persuading managers to take difficult assignments overseas. Companies with little international experience often make mistakes in these sorts of assignments. Statistically 60 per cent of expatriations fail and the main reason is the unhappiness of the spouse and family.

*Lead-in*
Discuss with your students whether they like/would like to work abroad. What problems would they encounter? Which countries would they like to work and live in and which would they prefer not to?

*Method*
(*See also* 'Stages of the activity – standard procedures', p. viii.)
1  After the lead-in discussion, look at the case itself.
2  Ask your students to read through the issue.
3  Make sure they all fully understand the case.
4  Assign roles (not only functional roles, but also a secretary to take minutes).
5  Allow 5 minutes to read through, prepare roles and language (*see* pp. viii–ix).
6  Agree on the timing for the meeting.
7  Run the meeting (audio- or video-record it if possible).
8  Give the students language and communication feedback.

*Follow-up*
(*See also* 'How to . . . write an output document', p. x.)
The group could draw up written policy guidelines for the company.

*Key vocabulary*
accompanied/unaccompanied
assignment
cross-cultural training
fast-track promotion
holiday entitlement
salary/expenses/allowances
to compensate
to ear-mark
working conditions

## Case study 11

### *International joint venture*

*Introduction*
This case deals with the problems of entering a new market. It also illustrates the difficulties for large global companies to succeed locally.

*Lead-in*
Discuss how large companies can best respond to local conditions. What alternatives are there to joint ventures as ways of entering a new market?

*Method*
(*See also* 'Stages of the activity – standard procedures', p. viii.)
1  After the lead-in discussion, look at the case itself.
2  Ask your students to read through the issue.
3  Make sure they all fully understand the case.
4  Assign roles (not only functional roles, but also a secretary to take minutes).
5  Allow 5 minutes to read through, prepare roles and language (*see* pp. viii–ix).
6  Agree on the timing for the meeting.
7  Run the meeting (audio- or video-record it if possible).
8  Give the students language and communication feedback.

*Follow-up*
(*See also* 'How to . . . write an output document', p. x.)
The written agenda should be finalized.

*Key vocabulary*
cash flow
goodwill
joint venture
royalty
sales office
subsidiary
target – to be above/below/on target
to enter a market
to invest
to pull out
turnover

*Teacher's notes*

## Case study 12

### Managing the project

*Introduction*

This case deals with the tensions between members of a team and the ways to resolve them. The underlying philosophy of team-working is that a well-balanced team can achieve, through combined efforts, more than is possible through the individual efforts of the members. However, it is important to get the team balance right. Imbalanced teams are unproductive in results and destructive to their members.

*Lead-in*

Warm up the group by discussing:

- their experience of working on projects
- their experience of team-working
- the requirements of high-performing teams
- the results of poorly constituted teams.

*Method*

(*See also* 'Stages of the activity – standard procedures', p. viii.)

1 After the lead-in discussion, look at the case itself.
2 Ask your students to read through the issue.
3 Make sure they all fully understand the case.
4 Assign roles (not only functional roles, but also a secretary to take minutes).
5 Allow 5 minutes to read through, prepare roles and language (*see* pp. viii–ix).
6 Agree on the timing for the meeting.
7 Run the meeting (audio- or video-record it if possible).
8 Give the students language and communication feedback.

*Follow-up*

(*See also* 'How to . . . write an output document', p. x.)
This type of case lends itself to written follow-up in the form of guidelines for managing projects.

*Key vocabulary*

challenge
creative – creativity – creative force
deadline
delay
edge – to have the edge – to lose the edge
effort – to make an effort
endeavour
innovative – innovation
inspiration
overrun
overtime

## Case study 13

### The millennium meeting

*Introduction*

The millennium will be celebrated in different ways around the globe. This case looks at a number of competing projects which aim to make a lasting impression on a local community. The discussion will centre around the utility of different initiatives in order to decide which one(s) to contribute to.

*Lead-in*

Warm up the group by discussing:

- how the millennium will be celebrated in their country/ies
- how the millennium should be celebrated
- whether money should be spent on helping groups within the community
- what types of initiatives they favour.

*Method*

(*See also* 'Stages of the activity – standard procedures', p. viii.)

1 After the lead-in discussion, look at the case itself.
2 Ask your students to read through the issue.
3 Make sure they all fully understand the case.
4 Assign roles (not only functional roles, but also a secretary to take minutes).
5 Allow 5 minutes to read through, prepare roles and language (*see* pp. viii–ix).
6 Agree on the timing for the meeting.
7 Run the meeting (audio- or video-record it if possible).
8 Give the students language and communication feedback.

*Follow-up*

(*See also* 'How to . . . write an output document', p. x.)
This type of case lends itself to written follow-up in the form of:

- minutes of the meeting
- an action plan for spending the fund
- a letter to the chosen recipient(s).

*Key vocabulary*

charity – charitable contribution
landmark
to fund – a fund
to raise the company's profile
to sleep rough
to sponsor – a sponsor – sponsorship
to support
worthy – worthy cause

*Teacher's notes*

## Case study 14

### *Multicultural project*

*Introduction*
This case centres around cross-cultural issues. Many companies find project teams are now composed of staff from different countries. A project therefore sharpens the focus on differences in working practices. This is particularly true where there are big time pressures.

*Lead-in*
Discuss attitudes towards time (punctuality, the working day, etc.), meetings (formality, length, etc.) and written communication (how much is written down) inside the organizations your students know.

*Method*
(*See also* 'Stages of the activity – standard procedures', p. viii.)
1 After the lead-in discussion, look at the case itself.
2 Ask your students to read through the issue.
3 Make sure they all fully understand the case.
4 Assign roles (not only functional roles, but also a secretary to take minutes).
5 Allow 5 minutes to read through, prepare roles and language (*see* pp. viii–ix).
6 Agree on the timing for the meeting.
7 Run the meeting (audio- or video-record it if possible).
8 Give the students language and communication feedback.

*Follow-up*
(*See also* 'How to . . . write an output document', p. x.)
Following the meeting, written minutes or a memo with recommendations could be written.

*Key vocabulary*
hierarchy – hierarchical – flat
meetings – chairing – minutes
reports – memos – agendas – minutes
time – deadline – milestone – to come in on time

## Case study 15

### *New technology*

*Introduction*
New technology refers to the use of computers for processing large quantities of information. The speed with which computers can handle data has made them a vital tool in every company. However, their widespread use has led to drawbacks. This case provides an opportunity to explore the advantages and disadvantages of computer use and the practical problems associated with supporting computer users.

*Lead-in*
Warm up the group by discussing:
- what they use their computers for
- how much time they spend in front of their computers
- how necessary computers are
- how they see the future uses of new technology in their jobs.

*Method*
(*See also* 'Stages of the activity – standard procedures', p. viii.)
1 After the lead-in discussion, look at the case itself.
2 Ask your students to read through the issue.
3 Make sure they all fully understand the case.
4 Assign roles (not only functional roles, but also a secretary to take minutes).
5 Allow 5 minutes to read through, prepare roles and language (*see* pp. viii–ix).
6 Agree on the timing for the meeting.
7 Run the meeting (audio- or video-record it if possible).
8 Give the students language and communication feedback.

*Follow-up*
(*See also* 'How to . . . write an output document', p. x.)
This type of case lends itself to written follow-up in the form of:
- minutes of the meeting
- guidelines for more effective computer use in the company.

*Key vocabulary*
computer application
survey
to analyse – analysis
to disrupt – disruption
to install . . . a computer
to keep track of
to process orders – to process purchases
to upgrade the system

*Teacher's notes*

## Case study 16

### *Outsourcing*

*Introduction*

Outsourcing is contracting out jobs or tasks which are not central to a company's core activities. It is one of the measures that companies have adopted to reduce costs and improve efficiency. This case deals with the outsourcing of cleaning services. In the past the company had employed its own cleaners. It now proposes to use the services of an external cleaning company. The dilemma is human, financial and practical, and the meeting should address all these questions.

*Lead-in*

Warm up the group by discussing:

- their experience of outsourcing in their companies
- the benefits and drawbacks of outsourcing.

*Method*

(*See also* 'Stages of the activity – standard procedures', p. viii.)

1. After the lead-in discussion, look at the case itself.
2. Ask your students to read through the issue.
3. Make sure they all fully understand the case.
4. Assign roles (not only functional roles, but also a secretary to take minutes).
5. Allow 5 minutes to read through, prepare roles and language (*see* pp. viii–ix).
6. Agree on the timing for the meeting.
7. Run the meeting (audio- or video-record it if possible).
8. Give the students language and communication feedback.

*Follow-up*

(*See also* 'How to . . . write an output document', p. x.)
This type of case lends itself to written follow-up in the form of:

- minutes of the meeting
- a letter to Mavis and Bill confirming the company's decision
- a statement of company policy on outsourcing.

*Key vocabulary*

labour relations
loyal
morale
shift
shop-floor – shop-floor workers
stake
to outsource – outsourcing
to subcontract
workforce

## Case study 17

### *Pay versus benefits*

*Introduction*

Benefits covers the rewards given to employees for their services to the company. The case concerns the balance between financial and non-financial remuneration in order to provide a balance between the employees' needs and company's needs.

*Lead-in*

Warm up the group by discussing:

- what types of benefits are paid/given by local companies
- the balance between financial and non-financial benefits
- the motivational effects of benefits.

*Method*

(*See also* 'Stages of the activity – standard procedures', p. viii.)

1. After the lead-in discussion, look at the case itself.
2. Ask your students to read through the issue.
3. Make sure they all fully understand the case.
4. Assign roles (not only functional roles, but also a secretary to take minutes).
5. Allow 5 minutes to read through, prepare roles and language (*see* pp. viii–ix).
6. Agree on the timing for the meeting.
7. Run the meeting (audio- or video-record it if possible).
8. Give the students language and communication feedback.

*Follow-up*

(*See also* 'How to . . . write an output document', p. x.)
This type of case lends itself to written follow-up in the form of:

- minutes of the meeting
- a policy document outlining the company's position.

*Key vocabulary*

bonus
insurance – assurance
payroll
remuneration – remuneration package
salary
to subsidize – subsidized lunches
wage

*Teacher's notes*

## Case study 18

### *Quality*

*Introduction*

This case raises questions about the importance of systematizing quality control. Many medium- to large-sized companies have gone for ISO 9000 accreditation as a way of institutionalizing quality management throughout their company. For small companies the cost of getting accreditation is relatively higher.

*Lead-in*

Discuss what is meant by quality. Are your students familiar with Total Quality Management (TQM), an approach to quality developed in the late 1970s?

*Method*

(*See also* 'Stages of the activity – standard procedures', p. viii.)

1 After the lead-in discussion, look at the case itself.
2 Ask your students to read through the issue.
3 Make sure they all fully understand the case.
4 Assign roles (not only functional roles, but also a secretary to take minutes).
5 Allow 5 minutes to read through, prepare roles and language (*see* pp. viii–ix).
6 Agree on the timing for the meeting.
7 Run the meeting (audio- or video-record it if possible).
8 Give the students language and communication feedback.

*Follow-up*

(*See also* 'How to . . . write an output document', p. x.)
Minutes or a memo.

*Key vocabulary*

check-lists
documentation
systems
to accredit – accreditation
to approve – a stamp of approval
to assess

## Case study 19

### *Relocation*

*Introduction*

This case centres around the problems of relocating a company. The trend to relocate away from metropolitan centres has been world-wide, so your students should be familiar with the issues.

*Lead-in*

Ask your students where they would prefer to work

- in the city/in the country?
- in the capital/in the regions?

*Method*

(*See also* 'Stages of the activity – standard procedures', p. viii.)

1 After the lead-in discussion, look at the case itself.
2 Ask your students to read through the issue.
3 Make sure they all fully understand the case.
4 Assign roles (not only functional roles, but also a secretary to take minutes).
5 Allow 5 minutes to read through, prepare roles and language (*see* pp. viii–ix).
6 Agree on the timing for the meeting.
7 Run the meeting (audio- or video-record it if possible).
8 Give the students language and communication feedback.

*Follow-up*

(*See also* 'How to . . . write an output document', p. x.)

1 Draw up a written action plan.
2 Then draft a memo to all staff informing them of the decision.

*Key vocabulary*

accommodation
lifestyle
removal
staff cuts
cost of living
to relocate – relocation – relocation budget
to spread rumours

*Teacher's notes*

## Case study 20

### Reorganization

*Introduction*
Delayering is a fashionable way of reorganizing a company. Recently there has been a move away from hierarchical pyramid structures to flat and lean organizations. Supposedly decisions are made more quickly, staff feel more involved and companies work more efficiently.

*Lead-in*
Ask your students how many employers they expect to have during a lifetime. Do they expect a continual rise in salary throughout their careers? What do they feel about sharing offices?

*Method*
(*See also* 'Stages of the activity – standard procedures', p. viii.)
1 After the lead-in discussion, look at the case itself.
2 Ask your students to read through the issue.
3 Make sure they all fully understand the case.
4 Assign roles (not only functional roles, but also a secretary to take minutes).
5 Allow 5 minutes to read through, prepare roles and language (*see* pp. viii–ix).
6 Agree on the timing for the meeting.
7 Run the meeting (audio- or video-record it if possible).
8 Give the students language and communication feedback.

*Follow-up*
(*See also* 'How to . . . write an output document', p. x.)
Minutes or a memo.

*Key vocabulary*
early retirement
flat
lean
open-plan office
redundancy (compulsory, voluntary)
salary cut/reduction
salary grade
to delayer
to downsize
to make somebody redundant

## Case study 21

### The safety committee

*Introduction*
This case focuses on safety issues. The tension in the meeting is created by reconciling two conflicting needs of the company: to save money and to implement safety measures.

*Lead-in*
Discuss with your students any recent industrial accidents. What do they think are the main causes of industrial accidents?

*Method*
(*See also* 'Stages of the activity – standard procedures', p. viii.)
1 After the lead-in discussion, look at the case itself.
2 Ask your students to read through the issue.
3 Make sure they all fully understand the case.
4 Assign roles (not only functional roles, but also a secretary to take minutes).
5 Allow 5 minutes to read through, prepare roles and language (*see* pp. viii–ix).
6 Agree on the timing for the meeting.
7 Run the meeting (audio- or video-record it if possible).
8 Give the students language and communication feedback.

*Follow-up*
(*See also* 'How to . . . write an output document', p. x.)
The recommendations should be written out.

*Key vocabulary*
lighting – badly-lit/well-lit
safety versus security
to convert – a conversion
to cut costs
to implement a recommendation
to sideline

*Teacher's notes*

## Case study 22

*Teleworking*

*Introduction*
Teleworking means working from home. Companies seeking to find alternatives ways of working and reducing costs have found that teleworking offers attractive possibilities to the company and the employee. However, it has its drawbacks. This case explores the positive and negative aspects of teleworking for the company and its employees in human, technical and financial terms.

*Lead-in*
Warm up the group by discussing:
- their experience of teleworking
- the advantages of teleworking
- the disadvantages of teleworking
- if they think the practice of teleworking will grow in their business area.

*Method*
(*See also* 'Stages of the activity – standard procedures', p. viii.)
1 After the lead-in discussion, look at the case itself.
2 Ask your students to read through the issue.
3 Make sure they all fully understand the case.
4 Assign roles (not only functional roles, but also a secretary to take minutes).
5 Allow 5 minutes to read through, prepare roles and language (*see* pp. viii–ix).
6 Agree on the timing for the meeting.
7 Run the meeting (audio- or video-record it if possible).
8 Give the students language and communication feedback.

*Follow-up*
(*See also* 'How to . . . write an output document', p. x.)
This type of case lends itself to written follow-up in the form of a policy statement about teleworking.

*Key vocabulary*
autonomous
communication – interpersonal communication
isolation
overheads
telecommuting
teleworking
to outsource – outsourcing

## Case study 23

*Training weekend*

*Introduction*
This case centres on the clash between company and individual cultures. Many companies have invested in training to develop better team work. Not every employee likes working in a team.

*Lead-in*
Find out if any of your students have participated in training to develop better teamwork. Has it been a by-product of other types of training? What do they think about adventure/outdoor training being used to help develop teamwork?

*Method*
(*See also* 'Stages of the activity – standard procedures', p. viii.)
1 After the lead-in discussion, look at the case itself.
2 Ask your students to read through the issue.
3 Make sure they all fully understand the case.
4 Assign roles (not only functional roles, but also a secretary to take minutes).
5 Allow 5 minutes to read through, prepare roles and language (*see* pp. viii–ix).
6 Agree on the timing for the meeting.
7 Run the meeting (audio- or video-record it if possible).
8 Give the students language and communication feedback.

*Follow-up*
(*See also* 'How to . . . write an output document', p. x.)
Write a memo or guidelines concerning the training policy.

*Key vocabulary*
outdoor training
supportive
sympathetic
teamwork – team-building – team spirit
to develop people
to lose your temper
to waste time

*Teacher's notes*

## Case study 24
*Workload*

*Introduction*
Many managers have to work longer hours now than previously. This may be partly due to a cult of hard work, but is probably mainly to do with working in a more competitive environment.

*Lead-in*
Discuss what hours your students work. How do they balance time between home/personal life and work? Do they think it is efficient to work long hours?

*Method*
(*See also* 'Stages of the activity – standard procedures', p. viii.)
1 After the lead-in discussion, look at the case itself.
2 Ask your students to read through the issue.
3 Make sure they all fully understand the case.
4 Assign roles (not only functional roles, but also a secretary to take minutes).
5 Allow 5 minutes to read through, prepare roles and language (*see* pp. viii–ix).
6 Agree on the timing for the meeting.
7 Run the meeting (audio- or video-record it if possible).
8 Give the students language and communication feedback.

*Follow-up*
(*See also* 'How to . . . write an output document', p. x.)
The minutes of the meeting should record any action plan.

*Key vocabulary*
breaking point
hard-working
illness
lazy
lead times
stress
to take time off
working day

## Staff committee meeting 1

*Introduction*
This type of meeting provides a range of agenda items with no specific roles. In this way the students are encouraged to express their own views on the issues.

*Lead-in*
The issues are all accessible and need no specialist knowledge.

*Method*
(*See also* 'Stages of the activity – standard procedures', p. viii.)
1 Ask your students to skim through the notes to the agenda (5 minutes).
2 Assign or ask for volunteers for the following roles for each item (in other words, the chairman should change for each item):
 – a chairman
 – a secretary (to take the minutes)
 – an observer (optional role if you want someone to observe the meeting in terms of its effectiveness).
3 Decide on the time for each item (10 minutes should be sufficient).
4 Allow a further 10 minutes to prepare for the meeting. (*see* pp. viii–ix). Suggest the following procedure for each item:
 – introduce and clarify the issue
 – ask for opinions
 – seek consensus and make a decision.
5 Make sure the students don't only prepare for the item they are going to chair. They will be asked for their opinions on all the other items.
6 Hold the meeting.
7 You can either give language and communication feedback after each item or wait till the end.

*Follow-up*
(*See also* 'How to . . . write an output document', p. x.)
Minutes of the meeting (collected from the 'secretaries' for each item).

*Key vocabulary*
early retirement
'first come, first served'
job (temporary, permanent)
open-plan office
quiet area
racial abuse – a racist – racism
smoking area
to ban

*Teacher's notes*

## Staff committee meeting 2

*Introduction*
This type of meeting provides a range of agenda items with no specific roles. In this way the students are encouraged to express their own views on the issues.

*Lead-in*
The issues are all accessible and need no specialist knowledge.

*Method*
(*See also* 'Stages of the activity – standard procedures', p. viii.)
1 Ask your students to skim through the notes to the agenda (5 minutes).
2 Assign or ask for volunteers for the following roles for each item (in other words, the chairman should change for each item):
 – a chairman
 – a secretary (to take the minutes)
 – an observer (optional role if you want someone to observe the meeting in terms of its effectiveness).
3 Decide on the time for each item (10 minutes should be sufficient).
4 Allow a further 10 minutes to prepare for the meeting. (*see* pp. viii–ix). Suggest the following procedure for each item:
 – introduce and clarify the issue
 – ask for opinions
 – seek consensus and make a decision.
5 Make sure the students don't only prepare for the item they are going to chair. They will be asked for their opinions on all the other items.
6 Hold the meeting.
7 You can either give language and communication feedback after each item or wait till the end.

*Follow-up*
(*See also* 'How to . . . write an output document', p. x.)
Minutes of the meeting (collected from the 'secretaries' for each item).

*Key vocabulary*
canteen
shelter
absent – absenteeism
ageist – ageism
drain – drainage – a drainage pipe
loyal
middle aged
sick leave
sponsor – sponsorship
to renovate
to support a charity
to take time off

## Staff committee meeting 3

*Introduction*
This type of meeting provides a range of agenda items with no specific roles. In this way the students are encouraged to express their own views on the issues.

*Lead-in*
The issues are all accessible and need no specialist knowledge.

*Method*
(*See also* 'Stages of the activity – standard procedures', p. viii.)
1 Ask your students to skim through the notes to the agenda (5 minutes).
2 Assign or ask for volunteers for the following roles for each item (in other words, the chairman should change for each item):
 – a chairman
 – a secretary (to take the minutes)
 – an observer (optional role if you want someone to observe the meeting in terms of its effectiveness).
3 Decide on the time for each item (10 minutes should be sufficient).
4 Allow a further 10 minutes to prepare for the meeting. (*see* pp. viii–ix). Suggest the following procedure for each item:
 – introduce and clarify the issue
 – ask for opinions
 – seek consensus and make a decision.
5 Make sure the students don't only prepare for the item they are going to chair. They will be asked for their opinions on all the other items.
6 Hold the meeting.
7 You can either give language and communication feedback after each item or wait till the end.

*Follow-up*
(*See also* 'How to . . . write an output document', p. x.)
Minutes of the meeting (collected from the 'secretaries' for each item).

*Key vocabulary*
access to Internet
appraisal (performance, upward)
domestic/foreign product
good cause
orphanage
perk

*Teacher's notes*

to afford
to be at ease
to hold a party
to search on the Internet

## Staff committee meeting 4

### Introduction
This type of meeting provides a range of agenda items with no specific roles. In this way the students are encouraged to express their own views on the issues.

### Lead-in
The issues are all accessible and need no specialist knowledge.

### Method
(*See also* 'Stages of the activity – standard procedures', p. viii.)
1 Ask your students to skim through the notes to the agenda (5 minutes).
2 Assign or ask for volunteers for the following roles for each item (in other words, the chairman should change for each item):
 – a chairman
 – a secretary (to take the minutes)
 – an observer (optional role if you want someone to observe the meeting in terms of its effectiveness).
3 Decide on the time for each item (10 minutes should be sufficient).
4 Allow a further 10 minutes to prepare for the meeting. (*see* pp. viii–ix). Suggest the following procedure for each item:
 – introduce and clarify the issue
 – ask for opinions
 – seek consensus and make a decision.
5 Make sure the students don't only prepare for the item they are going to chair. They will be asked for their opinions on all the other items.
6 Hold the meeting.
7 You can either give language and communication feedback after each item or wait till the end.

### Follow-up
(*See also* 'How to . . . write an output document', p. x.)
Minutes of the meeting (collected from the 'secretaries' for each item).

### Key vocabulary
abuse – verbal abuse
charisma – charismatic
charity – charitable organization
convict
environment – environmental friendliness
pilfering
premises (p.)
racial harassment
relocation
shop-floor
smoothly
subsidy
to sponsor – sponsorship

## Staff committee meeting 5

### Introduction
This type of meeting provides a range of agenda items with no specific roles. In this way the students are encouraged to express their own views on the issues.

### Lead-in
The issues are all accessible and need no specialist knowledge.

### Method
(*See also* 'Stages of the activity – standard procedures', p. viii.)
1 Ask your students to skim through the notes to the agenda (5 minutes).
2 Assign or ask for volunteers for the following roles for each item (in other words, the chairman should change for each item):
 – a chairman
 – a secretary (to take the minutes)
 – an observer (optional role if you want someone to observe the meeting in terms of its effectiveness).
3 Decide on the time for each item (10 minutes should be sufficient).
4 Allow a further 10 minutes to prepare for the meeting. (*see* pp. viii–ix). Suggest the following procedure for each item:
 – introduce and clarify the issue
 – ask for opinions
 – seek consensus and make a decision.
5 Make sure the students don't only prepare for the item they are going to chair. They will be asked for their opinions on all the other items.
6 Hold the meeting.
7 You can either give language and communication feedback after each item or wait till the end.

### Follow-up
(*See also* 'How to . . . write an output document', p. x.)
Minutes of the meeting (collected from the 'secretaries' for each item).

*Teacher's notes*

*Key vocabulary*
casualty
competent
horrified
scepticism – sceptical
to get through
to sexually harass – sexual harassment
upset

## Staff committee meeting 6

*Introduction*
This type of meeting provides a range of agenda items with no specific roles. In this way the students are encouraged to express their own views on the issues.

*Lead-in*
The issues are all accessible and need no specialist knowledge.

*Method*
(*See also* 'Stages of the activity – standard procedures', p. viii.)
1 Ask your students to skim through the notes to the agenda (5 minutes).
2 Assign or ask for volunteers for the following roles for each item (in other words, the chairman should change for each item):
 – a chairman
 – a secretary (to take the minutes)
 – an observer (optional role if you want someone to observe the meeting in terms of its effectiveness).
3 Decide on the time for each item (10 minutes should be sufficient).
4 Allow a further 10 minutes to prepare for the meeting. (*see* pp. viii–ix). Suggest the following procedure for each item:
 – introduce and clarify the issue
 – ask for opinions
 – seek consensus and make a decision.
5 Make sure the students don't only prepare for the item they are going to chair. They will be asked for their opinions on all the other items.
6 Hold the meeting.
7 You can either give language and communication feedback after each item or wait till the end.

*Follow-up*
(*See also* 'How to . . . write an output document', p. x.)
Minutes of the meeting (collected from the 'secretaries' for each item).

*Key vocabulary*
disgusted
incompetent
libel
promotion
referee – reference
relieved
remark
row
statutory
subordinate
to appoint
to fire
to inherit
to offend – offensive

## Staff committee meeting 7

*Introduction*
This type of meeting provides a range of agenda items with no specific roles. In this way the students are encouraged to express their own views on the issues.

*Lead-in*
The issues are all accessible and need no specialist knowledge.

*Method*
(*See also* 'Stages of the activity – standard procedures', p. viii.)
1 Ask your students to skim through the notes to the agenda (5 minutes).
2 Assign or ask for volunteers for the following roles for each item (in other words, the chairman should change for each item):
 – a chairman
 – a secretary (to take the minutes)
 – an observer (optional role if you want someone to observe the meeting in terms of its effectiveness).
3 Decide on the time for each item (10 minutes should be sufficient).
4 Allow a further 10 minutes to prepare for the meeting. (*see* pp. viii–ix). Suggest the following procedure for each item:
 – introduce and clarify the issue
 – ask for opinions
 – seek consensus and make a decision.
5 Make sure the students don't only prepare for the item they are going to chair. They will be asked for their opinions on all the other items.
6 Hold the meeting.
7 You can either give language and communication feedback after each item or wait till the end.

*Teacher's notes*

*Follow-up*
(*See also* 'How to . . . write an output document', p. x.)
Minutes of the meeting (collected from the 'secretaries' for each item).

*Key vocabulary*
morale
overindulgence
rumour – to spread a rumour
speculation
subordinate
takeover
to cite
to contribute
to freelance – a freelance – freelancing
to take someone out

## Staff committee meeting 8

*Introduction*
This type of meeting provides a range of agenda items with no specific roles. In this way the students are encouraged to express their own views on the issues.

*Lead-in*
The issues are all accessible and need no specialist knowledge.

*Method*
(*See also* 'Stages of the activity – standard procedures', p. viii.)

1 Ask your students to skim through the notes to the agenda (5 minutes).
2 Assign or ask for volunteers for the following roles for each item (in other words, the chairman should change for each item):
   – a chairman
   – a secretary (to take the minutes)
   – an observer (optional role if you want someone to observe the meeting in terms of its effectiveness).
3 Decide on the time for each item (10 minutes should be sufficient).
4 Allow a further 10 minutes to prepare for the meeting. (*see* pp. viii–ix). Suggest the following procedure for each item:
   – introduce and clarify the issue
   – ask for opinions
   – seek consensus and make a decision.
5 Make sure the students don't only prepare for the item they are going to chair. They will be asked for their opinions on all the other items.
6 Hold the meeting.
7 You can either give language and communication feedback after each item or wait till the end.

*Follow-up*
(*See also* 'How to . . . write an output document', p. x.)
Minutes of the meeting (collected from the 'secretaries' for each item).

*Key vocabulary*
compensation
controversy
devastating
environmentalist
hype
irritation
leak
loan
reluctant
repetitive strain injury (RSI)
self-fulfilment
shareholder
tabloid newspaper
to approach
to cite
waste – waste treatment

*Teacher's notes*

## Specialist agenda 1

*Management*

*Introduction*
As this is the introductory agenda in the section of specialist agendas, it aims to draw on the students' own experiences in their professional area. The first agenda takes the broad field of management and explores the question: What is management? Anyone from a management background will be able to contribute.

*Lead-in*
Ask your students:
- what the tasks of a manager are
- what the attributes of a good manager are
- how far training helps to develop managers.

*Method*
(*See also* 'Stages of the activity – standard procedures', p. viii.)
1 After the lead-in discussion, look at the case itself.
2 Ask your students to read through the issue.
3 Make sure they all fully understand the problem.
4 Assign roles (not only functional roles, but also a secretary to take minutes).
5 Allow 5 minutes to read through, prepare roles and language (*see* pp. viii–ix).
6 Agree on the timing for the meeting (between 30 and 60 minutes).
7 Run the meeting (audio- or video-record it if possible).
8 Give the students language and communication feedback.

*Follow-up*
(*See also* 'How to . . . write an output document', p. x.)
Minutes

*Key vocabulary*
ambition
attitude
commitment
common sense
enthusiasm – enthusiastic
pride
sound
stability
to accomplish – accomplishment
to delegate – delegator – delegation
to forecast
to motivate – motivation

## Specialist agenda 2

*Quality*

*Introduction*
This type of agenda encourages the students to draw on their role and own experience in their professional area. This agenda focuses on the area of quality. In the eighties, many companies saw the quest for quality as a 'holy grail'. Today quality is still important, though it is recognized that there is a point at which trying to improve quality still further can be more expensive than the benefits. All managers are concerned with quality and should have something to say about this issue.

*Lead-in*
Ask your students:
- who looks after quality in their companies
- if quality is important for them
- how they ensure quality.

*Method*
(*See also* 'Stages of the activity – standard procedures', p. viii.)
1 After the lead-in discussion, look at the case itself.
2 Ask your students to read through the issue.
3 Make sure they all fully understand the problem.
4 Assign roles (not only functional roles, but also a secretary to take minutes).
5 Allow 5 minutes to read through, prepare roles and language (*see* pp. viii–ix).
6 Agree on the timing for the meeting (between 30 and 60 minutes).
7 Run the meeting (audio- or video-record it if possible).
8 Give the students language and communication feedback.

*Follow-up*
(*See also* 'How to . . . write an output document', p. x.)
Minutes

*Key vocabulary*
fairground
leisure – leisure industry – leisure pursuit
to cut corners – to cut costs
to favour
to reassure

*Teacher's notes*

## Specialist agenda 3

### Human resources (1)

*Introduction*
This type of agenda encourages the students to draw on their role and own experience in their own professional area. Every manager is involved in managing people and should have something to say about the scope and practice of human resources management.

*Lead-in*
Ask your students:

- if they have a human resources function in their company and what it is
- what the main human resource concerns are in their companies
- how these human concerns can best be handled.

*Method*
(*See also* 'Stages of the activity – standard procedures', p. viii.)

1 After the lead-in discussion, look at the case itself.
2 Ask your students to read through the issue.
3 Make sure they all fully understand the problem.
4 Assign roles (not only functional roles, but also a secretary to take minutes).
5 Allow 5 minutes to read through, prepare roles and language (*see* pp. viii–ix).
6 Agree on the timing for the meeting (between 30 and 60 minutes).
7 Run the meeting (audio- or video-record it if possible).
8 Give the students language and communication feedback.

*Follow-up*
(*See also* 'How to . . . write an output document', p. x.)
Minutes

*Key vocabulary*
bottom line
manpower
shareholder
to convene
to downsize – downsizing
to forsake
to optimize
to rationalize – rationalization
welfare
wide-ranging
workforce

## Specialist agenda 4

### Promotion

*Introduction*
This type of agenda encourages the students to draw on their role and own experience in their own professional area. This agenda focuses on promotion. Promotion concerns the different ways of raising the public's awareness of your products or services so that you can sell them more effectively. This agenda should be of interest to all managers involved in the fields of marketing and sales.

*Lead-in*
Ask your students:

- what methods of promotion are used by their companies to sell their products
- how successful these methods are
- which other promotional tools could be used to increase sales.

*Method*
(*See also* 'Stages of the activity – standard procedures', p. viii.)

1 After the lead-in discussion, look at the case itself.
2 Ask your students to read through the issue.
3 Make sure they all fully understand the problem.
4 Assign roles (not only functional roles, but also a secretary to take minutes).
5 Allow 5 minutes to read through, prepare roles and language (*see* pp. viii–ix).
6 Agree on the timing for the meeting (between 30 and 60 minutes).
7 Run the meeting (audio- or video-record it if possible).
8 Give the students language and communication feedback.

*Follow-up*
(*See also* 'How to . . . write an output document', p. x.)
Minutes

*Key vocabulary*
casual
perimeter advertising
personal selling
point-of-sale advertising
potential – potential customers – existing customers
promotion – promotional – promotional tool
to go to great lengths
to launch – a launch
to sponsor – sponsorship
to subscribe
workout

*Teacher's notes*

## Specialist agenda 5

### *The training dilemma*

*Introduction*

This type of agenda encourages the students to draw on their role and own experience in their own professional area. Companies need a competent, up-to-date and well-developed workforce. This requires training. But should this training be provided by in-house trainers, or should it be outsourced? This agenda focuses on the advantages and disadvantages of each approach. It should be of interest to people working in training and human resources.

*Lead-in*

Ask your students:

- about the range of training programmes offered by their companies
- whether training is provided by in-house or external trainers
- about the advantages and disadvantages of in-house vs. external trainers.

*Method*

(*See also* 'Stages of the activity – standard procedures', p. viii.)

1 After the lead-in discussion, look at the case itself.
2 Ask your students to read through the issue.
3 Make sure they all fully understand the problem.
4 Assign roles (not only functional roles, but also a secretary to take minutes).
5 Allow 5 minutes to read through, prepare roles and language (*see* pp. viii–ix).
6 Agree on the timing for the meeting (between 30 and 60 minutes).
7 Run the meeting (audio- or video-record it if possible).
8 Give the students language and communication feedback.

*Follow-up*

(*See also* 'How to . . . write an output document', p. x.)
Minutes

*Key vocabulary*

burnout
commitment – committed
generic
reliable
skill
to fail
to make redundant
to outsource

## Specialist agenda 6

### *Sales and marketing*

*Introduction*

This type of agenda encourages the students to draw on their role and own experience in the professional area. It focuses on an ethical issue related to advertising.

*Lead-in*

Ask your student about the type of advertisements they see. Do they ever cause offence? If so, for what reason? What type of ads do they like best? If you have access to a video-recorder, a very good lead-in would be to show a few sample TV commercials and ask your students for their opinions.

*Method*

(*See also* 'Stages of the activity – standard procedures', p. viii.)

1 After the lead-in discussion, look at the case itself.
2 Ask your students to read through the issue.
3 Make sure they all fully understand the problem.
4 Assign roles (not only functional roles, but also a secretary to take minutes).
5 Allow 5 minutes to read through, prepare roles and language (*see* pp. viii–ix).
6 Agree on the timing for the meeting (between 30 and 60 minutes).
7 Run the meeting (audio- or video-record it if possible).
8 Give the students language and communication feedback.

*Follow-up*

(*See also* 'How to . . . write an output document', p. x.)
Minutes

*Key vocabulary*

advertising agency
commercial (ad)
effective
over-dramatic
to apologize
to blow up out of proportion
to frighten
to offend someone/to cause offence (to someone)
to withdraw

*Teacher's notes*

## Specialist agenda 7

### Finance

*Introduction*
This agenda centres around some common financial problems for small- to medium-sized businesses. Anybody with a financial background will have something to say about these issues.

*Lead-in*
Discuss the role of finance in your students' workplaces. Is it central? Do all managers know and understand financial questions? What are the main financial issues facing their organizations?

*Method*
(*See also* 'Stages of the activity – standard procedures', p. viii.)
1 After the lead-in discussion, look at the case itself.
2 Ask your students to read through the issue.
3 Make sure they all fully understand the problem.
4 Assign roles (not only functional roles, but also a secretary to take minutes).
5 Allow 5 minutes to read through, prepare roles and language (*see* pp. viii–ix).
6 Agree on the timing for the meeting (between 30 and 60 minutes).
7 Run the meeting (audio- or video-record it if possible).
8 Give the students language and communication feedback.

*Follow-up*
(*See also* 'How to . . . write an output document', p. x.)
Minutes

*Key vocabulary*
bank charges
goodwill
itemized telephone bill
management accounts
nominal accounts
overheads/overhead costs
profit & loss account

## Specialist agenda 8

### Legal affairs

*Introduction*
This agenda presents a variety of legal items. Not all lawyers will face these precise problems but all will have something to say about them.

*Lead-in*
Discuss the role of the legal department in a company. What are its main responsibilities? What are its main areas of expertise?

*Method*
(*See also* 'Stages of the activity – standard procedures', p. viii.)
1 After the lead-in discussion, look at the case itself.
2 Ask your students to read through the issue.
3 Make sure they all fully understand the problem.
4 Assign roles (not only functional roles, but also a secretary to take minutes).
5 Allow 5 minutes to read through, prepare roles and language (*see* pp. viii–ix).
6 Agree on the timing for the meeting (between 30 and 60 minutes).
7 Run the meeting (audio- or video-record it if possible).
8 Give the students language and communication feedback.

*Follow-up*
(*See also* 'How to . . . write an output document', p. x.)
Minutes

*Key vocabulary*
commercial law
contractual law
insurance claim
law firm
legal expertise
to afford
to draft a contract
to draw up a contract

*Teacher's notes*

## Specialist agenda 9

### Human resources (2)

*Introduction*
This agenda presents three items which often concern human resources experts.

*Lead-in*
Discuss the role of the human resources department inside a company. What are its main responsibilities? What sort of problems does it face today?

*Method*
(*See also* 'Stages of the activity – standard procedures', p. viii.)
1 After the lead-in discussion, look at the case itself.
2 Ask your students to read through the issue.
3 Make sure they all fully understand the problem.
4 Assign roles (not only functional roles, but also a secretary to take minutes).
5 Allow 5 minutes to read through, prepare roles and language (*see* pp. viii–ix).
6 Agree on the timing for the meeting (between 30 and 60 minutes).
7 Run the meeting (audio- or video-record it if possible).
8 Give the students language and communication feedback.

*Follow-up*
(*See also* 'How to . . . write an output document', p. x.)
Minutes

*Key vocabulary*
celebration
fair balance
glass ceiling
duplication
efficient
inefficient
jobsharing
positive discrimination
staff morale
team-building

## Specialist agenda 10

### Production

*Introduction*
Production Managers will be familiar with these items which concern the management of production resources (time and people) and also a key production issue – safety.

*Lead-in*
Discuss the role of the production department inside a company. What are its main responsibilities? What sort of problems does it face today?

*Method*
(*See also* 'Stages of the activity – standard procedures', p. viii.)
1 After the lead-in discussion, look at the case itself.
2 Ask your students to read through the issue.
3 Make sure they all fully understand the problem.
4 Assign roles (not only functional roles, but also a secretary to take minutes).
5 Allow 5 minutes to read through, prepare roles and language (*see* pp. viii–ix).
6 Agree on the timing for the meeting (between 30 and 60 minutes).
7 Run the meeting (audio- or video-record it if possible).
8 Give the students language and communication feedback.

*Follow-up*
(*See also* 'How to . . . write an output document', p. x.)
Minutes

*Key vocabulary*
apprentice
break
first aider
monotonous work
rest-time
shift
staff turnover
to attend a course
to man a machine

Teacher's notes

## Decision-making 1

### Outsourcing or not?

*Introduction*

This type of agenda is designed to develop decision-making skills. It is important that the decision is made without resorting to voting.
This decision concerns whether to outsource a company's information technology (IT) activity or not.

*Lead-in*

Discuss the modern trend for outsourcing. What are its advantages and disadvantages?

*Method*

(*See also* 'Stages of the activity – standard procedures', p. viii.)

1 After the lead-in discussion, look at the case itself.
2 Ask your students to read through the issue.
3 Make sure they all fully understand the decision that has to be made.
4 Assign roles (not only functional roles, but also a secretary to take minutes).
5 Allow 5 minutes to read through, prepare roles and language (*see* pp. viii–ix).
6 Agree on the timing for the meeting (approx. 45 minutes).
7 Run the meeting (audio- or video-record it if possible).
8 Give the students language and communication feedback.

*Follow-up*

(*See also* 'How to . . . write an output document', p. x.)
Minutes

*Key vocabulary*

confidential
know-how
on-site
payroll
security
tender – to tender
to invest – investment
to maintain – maintenance
to outsource
to take over
to upgrade

## Decision-making 2

### New training manager

*Introduction*

This type of agenda is designed to develop decision-making skills. It is important that the decision is made without resorting to voting.
This decision concerns the recruitment of a new training manager.

*Lead-in*

Discuss the process of recruitment. What are the difficulties in recruiting the right person? What is the best method/process of selection?

*Method*

(*See also* 'Stages of the activity – standard procedures', p. viii.)

1 After the lead-in discussion, look at the case itself.
2 Ask your students to read through the issue.
3 Make sure they all fully understand the decision that has to be made.
4 Assign roles (not only functional roles, but also a secretary to take minutes).
5 Allow 5 minutes to read through, prepare roles and language (*see* pp. viii–ix).
6 Agree on the timing for the meeting (approx. 45 minutes).
7 Run the meeting (audio- or video-record it if possible).
8 Give the students language and communication feedback.

*Follow-up*

(*See also* 'How to . . . write an output document', p. x.)
Minutes

*Key vocabulary*

experience – limited experience
hobbies
interests
marital status
personality:
    ambitious
    bright
    conscientious
    dynamic
    easy-going
    intelligent
    personable
qualifications – well-qualified/poorly-qualified

*Teacher's notes*

## Decision-making 3

### The budget

*Introduction*
This type of agenda is designed to develop decision-making skills. It is important that the decision is made without resorting to voting.
This decision concerns the cuts in departmental budgets.

*Lead-in*
Discuss the difficulties of prioritizing cuts in budgets. How do you choose between cutting the training budget and the information technology (IT) budget?

*Method*
(*See also* 'Stages of the activity – standard procedures', p. viii.)
1 After the lead-in discussion, look at the case itself.
2 Ask your students to read through the issue.
3 Make sure they all fully understand the decision that has to be made.
4 Assign roles (not only functional roles, but also a secretary to take minutes).
5 Allow 5 minutes to read through, prepare roles and language (*see* pp. viii–ix).
6 Agree on the timing for the meeting (approx. 45 minutes).
7 Run the meeting (audio- or video-record it if possible).
8 Give the students language and communication feedback.

*Follow-up*
(*See also* 'How to . . . write an output document', p. x.)
Minutes

*Key vocabulary*
desktop systems
in-house course
overheads
redecoration
refurbishment
refurnishing
sales promotion event
target – below/above/on target
to boost corporate image
to support sales

## Problem-solving 1

### Time management

*Introduction*
This agenda is designed for quick access. There is very little briefing required. It should encourage a creative meeting in which everybody is encouraged to give opinions.
This problem centres on how mangers spend their time.

*Lead-in*
Ask your students how they spend their time. Ask them to draw a pie chart showing how their time is used.

*Method*
(*See also* 'Stages of the activity – standard procedures', p. viii.)
1 After the lead-in discussion, look at the problem itself.
2 Ask your students to read through the issue.
3 Make sure they all fully understand the problem.
4 Assign roles (chairman, secretary).
5 Allow 2 minutes to prepare (*see* pp. viii–ix).
6 Agree on the timing for the meeting (approx. 20 minutes).
7 Run the meeting (audio- or video-record it if possible).
8 Give the students language and communication feedback.

*Follow-up*
(*See also* 'How to . . . write an output document', p. x.)
Minutes of the meeting (including action plan).

*Key vocabulary*
meetings:
   effective
   fruitful
   ineffective
   long-winded
   productive
   talking shop
   time consuming
time:
   to fill the time
   to run out of time
   to shorten the time
   to waste time

*Teacher's notes*

## Problem-solving 2

### Staff morale

*Introduction*

This agenda is designed for quick access. There is very little briefing required. It should encourage a creative meeting in which everybody is encouraged to give opinions.

This problem centres on how to improve staff morale.

*Lead-in*

Ask your students how much job satisfaction they get. What factors affect job satisfaction most?

*Method*

(*See also* 'Stages of the activity – standard procedures', p. viii.)

1. After the lead-in discussion, look at the problem itself.
2. Ask your students to read through the issue.
3. Make sure they all fully understand the problem.
4. Assign roles (chairman, secretary).
5. Allow 2 minutes to prepare (*see* pp. viii–ix).
6. Agree on the timing for the meeting (approx. 20 minutes).
7. Run the meeting (audio- or video-record it if possible).
8. Give the students language and communication feedback.

*Follow-up*

(*See also* 'How to . . . write an output document', p. x.)
Minutes of the meeting (including action plan).

*Key vocabulary*

clear accountability/responsibility
job description
performance appraisal
profit sharing
satisfaction – to be satisfied
team-building
to enjoy/don't mind/hate/can't stand

## Problem-solving 3

### Personality clash

*Introduction*

This agenda is designed for quick access. There is very little briefing required. It should encourage a creative meeting in which everybody is encouraged to give opinions.

This problem centres on an employee who does not fit into the organization.

*Lead-in*

Ask your students whether they have any colleagues who they don't get on with. How can personality clashes best be solved at work?

*Method*

(*See also* 'Stages of the activity – standard procedures', p. viii.)

1. After the lead-in discussion, look at the problem itself.
2. Ask your students to read through the issue.
3. Make sure they all fully understand the problem.
4. Assign roles (chairman, secretary).
5. Allow 2 minutes to prepare (*see* pp. viii–ix).
6. Agree on the timing for the meeting (approx. 20 minutes).
7. Run the meeting (audio- or video-record it if possible).
8. Give the students language and communication feedback.

*Follow-up*

(*See also* 'How to . . . write an output document', p. x.)
Minutes of the meeting (including action plan).

*Key vocabulary*

arrogant
demotion
distant
extrovert
introvert
promotion
to get on with someone
to mix with people
transfer

*Teacher's notes*

## Problem-solving 4

*Working time and lunch time*

*Introduction*
This agenda is designed for quick access. There is very little briefing required. It should encourage a creative meeting in which everybody is encouraged to give opinions.
This agenda centres on the problem of organizing work time in order to complete all the tasks that need doing.

*Lead-in*
Ask your students:

- if they or their office staff have to take a lunch break and for how long
- if they think it's a good idea to have a break from work at lunch time
- whether their companies allow office staff to eat and drink in their offices.

*Method*
(*See also* 'Stages of the activity – standard procedures', p. viii.)
1 After the lead-in discussion, look at the problem itself.
2 Ask your students to read through the issue.
3 Make sure they all fully understand the problem.
4 Assign roles (chairman, secretary).
5 Allow 2 minutes to prepare (*see* pp. viii–ix).
6 Agree on the timing for the meeting (approx. 20 minutes).
7 Run the meeting (audio- or video-record it if possible).
8 Give the students language and communication feedback.

*Follow-up*
(*See also* 'How to . . . write an output document', p. x.)
Minutes of the meeting (including action plan).

*Key vocabulary*
canteen
clerk – clerical staff
morale
to ban – a ban
to spill – spillage
to suit

## Problem-solving 5

*Use of the Internet*

*Introduction*
This agenda is designed for quick access. There is very little briefing required. It should encourage a creative meeting in which everybody is encouraged to give opinions.
This problem centres on whether the use of Internet needs more control to prevent private access at the company's expense.

*Lead-in*
Ask your students:

- if they use Internet for professional purposes from their offices
- if there is any control over Internet use
- if there should be any control over Internet use.

*Method*
(*See also* 'Stages of the activity – standard procedures', p. viii.)
1 After the lead-in discussion, look at the problem itself.
2 Ask your students to read through the issue.
3 Make sure they all fully understand the problem.
4 Assign roles (chairman, secretary).
5 Allow 2 minutes to prepare (*see* pp. viii–ix).
6 Agree on the timing for the meeting (approx. 20 minutes).
7 Run the meeting (audio- or video-record it if possible).
8 Give the students language and communication feedback.

*Follow-up*
(*See also* 'How to . . . write an output document', p. x.)
Minutes of the meeting (including action plan).

*Key vocabulary*
chat line – sex line
fuss
gesture
initiative
Internet site
to search for – to search for leads – to search for contacts
to surf the net – to access the net
to wear off

*Teacher's notes*

## Problem-solving 6

### Poaching

*Introduction*

This agenda is designed for quick access. There is very little briefing required. It should encourage a creative meeting in which everybody is encouraged to give opinions.

This problem centres on the ethical issue of poaching and the practical concerns of confidentiality of information.

*Lead-in*

Ask your students:

- if head-hunting and poaching are common practice in their business community
- if companies should behave (more) ethically when recruiting managers.

*Method*

(*See also* 'Stages of the activity – standard procedures', p. viii.)

1 After the lead-in discussion, look at the problem itself.
2 Ask your students to read through the issue.
3 Make sure they all fully understand the problem.
4 Assign roles (chairman, secretary).
5 Allow 2 minutes to prepare (*see* pp. viii–ix).
6 Agree on the timing for the meeting (approx. 20 minutes).
7 Run the meeting (audio- or video-record it if possible).
8 Give the students language and communication feedback.

*Follow-up*

(*See also* 'How to . . . write an output document', p. x.)
Minutes of the meeting (including action plan).

*Key vocabulary*

predecessor
rival – rivalry
ruthless
scandal
to head-hunt – head-hunting – head-hunter
to poach – poaching
to steer
to tempt
underhand
vacant – vacant post

## Problem-solving 7

### Delegation

*Introduction*

This agenda is designed for quick access. There is very little briefing required. It should encourage a creative meeting in which everybody is encouraged to give opinions.

This problem centres on how to delegate tasks effectively.

*Lead-in*

Ask your students:

- what types of task they delegate
- how to delegate effectively.

*Method*

(*See also* 'Stages of the activity – standard procedures', p. viii.)

1 After the lead-in discussion, look at the problem itself.
2 Ask your students to read through the issue.
3 Make sure they all fully understand the problem.
4 Assign roles (chairman, secretary).
5 Allow 2 minutes to prepare (*see* pp. viii–ix).
6 Agree on the timing for the meeting (approx. 20 minutes).
7 Run the meeting (audio- or video-record it if possible).
8 Give the students language and communication feedback.

*Follow-up*

(*See also* 'How to . . . write an output document', p. x.)
Minutes of the meeting (including action plan).

*Key vocabulary*

covering letter
feedback
overrated
routine
subordinate
to delegate
trust – to gain trust

*Teacher's notes*

## Problem-solving 8

### *Open-plan*

*Introduction*

This agenda is designed for quick access. There is very little briefing required. It should encourage a creative meeting in which everybody is encouraged to give opinions.
This problem centres on how to use office space most efficiently.

*Lead-in*

Ask your students:

- if their companies have a facilities manager to look after premises
- if they have any experience of open-plan offices
- if their companies use their office space efficiently.

*Method*

(*See also* 'Stages of the activity – standard procedures', p. viii.)

1 After the lead-in discussion, look at the problem itself.
2 Ask your students to read through the issue.
3 Make sure they all fully understand the problem.
4 Assign roles (chairman, secretary).
5 Allow 2 minutes to prepare (*see* pp. viii–ix).
6 Agree on the timing for the meeting (approx. 20 minutes).
7 Run the meeting (audio- or video-record it if possible).
8 Give the students language and communication feedback.

*Follow-up*

(*See also* 'How to . . . write an output document', p. x.)
Minutes of the meeting (including action plan).

*Key vocabulary*

open-plan
preliminary
security
survey
to acquire – acquisition
to disrupt – disruption
to renovate – renovation

## Problem-solving 9

### *Training course vs. on-the-job training*

*Introduction*

This agenda is designed for quick access. There is very little briefing required. It should encourage a creative meeting in which everybody is encouraged to give opinions.
This problem centres on the role of training in an organization, how to provide it and, specifically, how to develop leadership skills.

*Lead-in*

Ask your students:

- what training courses they have been on recently
- if they were trained on training courses or on the job
- the advantages and disadvantages of each training mode.

*Method*

(*See also* 'Stages of the activity – standard procedures', p. viii.)

1 After the lead-in discussion, look at the problem itself.
2 Ask your students to read through the issue.
3 Make sure they all fully understand the problem.
4 Assign roles (chairman, secretary).
5 Allow 2 minutes to prepare (*see* pp. viii–ix).
6 Agree on the timing for the meeting (approx. 20 minutes).
7 Run the meeting (audio- or video-record it if possible).
8 Give the students language and communication feedback.

*Follow-up*

(*See also* 'How to . . . write an output document', p. x.)
Minutes of the meeting (including action plan).

*Key vocabulary*

challenge
exhausted
nightmare
ostensibly
reluctantly
to appoint
to encounter – an encounter – an encounter weekend
to threaten

*Teacher's notes*

## Problem-solving 10

### *Employment of disabled people*

*Introduction*
This agenda is designed for quick access. There is very little briefing required. It should encourage a creative meeting in which everybody is encouraged to give opinions.
This problem centres on balancing the principle of employing disabled people with the practical considerations.

*Lead-in*
Ask your students:
- if their company has a policy on employing disabled people
- if companies should try to integrate disabled people more
- what steps should be taken to achieve this.

*Method*
(*See also* 'Stages of the activity – standard procedures', p. viii.)
1 After the lead-in discussion, look at the problem itself.
2 Ask your students to read through the issue.
3 Make sure they all fully understand the problem.
4 Assign roles (chairman, secretary).
5 Allow 2 minutes to prepare (*see* pp. viii–ix).
6 Agree on the timing for the meeting (approx. 20 minutes).
7 Run the meeting (audio- or video-record it if possible).
8 Give the students language and communication feedback.

*Follow-up*
(*See also* 'How to . . . write an output document', p. x.)
Minutes of the meeting (including action plan).

*Key vocabulary*
caring employer
circuit board
disabled
false economy
layoff
payroll
redundancy
to be stretched
to load
to match
to package
to subsidize – subsidy
wage

## Problem-solving 11

### *Recycling*

*Introduction*
This agenda is designed for quick access. There is very little briefing required. It should encourage a creative meeting in which everybody is encouraged to give opinions.
This problem centres on balancing the environmental issue of recycling with the costs.

*Lead-in*
Ask your students:
- about their experience of recycling
- if their company recycles paper, plastic, glass, etc.
- what steps their companies should take to become more environmentally aware.

*Method*
(*See also* 'Stages of the activity – standard procedures', p. viii.)
1 After the lead-in discussion, look at the problem itself.
2 Ask your students to read through the issue.
3 Make sure they all fully understand the problem.
4 Assign roles (chairman, secretary).
5 Allow 2 minutes to prepare (*see* pp. viii–ix).
6 Agree on the timing for the meeting (approx. 20 minutes).
7 Run the meeting (audio- or video-record it if possible).
8 Give the students language and communication feedback.

*Follow-up*
(*See also* 'How to . . . write an output document', p. x.)
Minutes of the meeting (including action plan).

*Key vocabulary*
bin
garbage – rubbish – waste
glut
to boost
to consume – consumer – consumerist
to recycle – recycling
to waver

*Teacher's notes*

## Problem-solving 12

### *An attractive remuneration package*

*Introduction*
This agenda is designed for quick access. There is very little briefing required. It should encourage a creative meeting in which everybody is encouraged to give opinions.
This problem centres on how to attract the right person to the job and the type of rewards to be offered.

*Lead-in*
Ask your students:

- what motivates managers
- how important money is in the equation
- whether more money attracts better people.

*Method*
(*See also* 'Stages of the activity – standard procedures', p. viii.)
1 After the lead-in discussion, look at the problem itself.
2 Ask your students to read through the issue.
3 Make sure they all fully understand the problem.
4 Assign roles (chairman, secretary).
5 Allow 2 minutes to prepare (*see* pp. viii–ix).
6 Agree on the timing for the meeting (approx. 20 minutes).
7 Run the meeting (audio- or video-record it if possible).
8 Give the students language and communication feedback.

*Follow-up*
(*See also* 'How to . . . write an output document', p. x.)
Minutes of the meeting (including action plan).

*Key vocabulary*
audit
pension
remuneration
the golden years
to envisage
to recruit

## Strategy meeting 1

### *Mission statement*

*Introduction*
This agenda is based around a strategic business issue. The meeting will decide how to tackle the issue and the participants will write a document after the meeting decisions have been taken.
The issue concerns the contents of a mission statement and the writing task is to draft a mission statement.

*Lead-in*
Ask your students:

- if their company has a mission statement
- the purpose of a mission statement
- the audience for the mission statement
- how important it is for companies to have their own mission statement.

*Method*
(*See also* 'Stages of the activity – standard procedures', p. viii.)
1 After the lead-in discussion, look at the problem itself.
2 Ask your students to read through the issue.
3 Make sure they all fully understand the problem.
4 Assign roles (chairman, secretary).
5 Allow 2 minutes to prepare (*see* pp. viii–ix).
6 Agree on the timing for the meeting (approx. 20 minutes).
7 Run the meeting (audio- or video-record it if possible).
8 Give the students language and communication feedback.

*Follow-up*
(*See also* 'How to . . . write an output document', p. x.)

- Organize groups for writing task.
- Give a time limit for drafting the mission statement.
- Give the students language and communication feedback on writing.

*Key vocabulary*
conduct
customer focus
integrity
lead time
lean
scandal
shareholder
slim
stakeholder
to downsize
to streamline

*Teacher's notes*

## Strategy meeting 2

### Job advertisement

*Introduction*
This agenda is based around a strategic business issue. The meeting will decide how to tackle the issue and the participants will write a document after the meeting decisions have been taken.
The issue concerns how to recruit a number of new employees and the writing task is to draft the advertisements or requirements for the positions.

*Lead-in*
Ask your students:

- if they have been involved in recruitment
- where and how their companies find white-collar workers
- where and how their companies find blue-collar workers
- if these are the best methods and the best sources.

*Method*
(*See also* 'Stages of the activity – standard procedures', p. viii.)

1 After the lead-in discussion, look at the problem itself.
2 Ask your students to read through the issue.
3 Make sure they all fully understand the problem.
4 Assign roles (chairman, secretary).
5 Allow 2 minutes to prepare (*see* pp. viii–ix).
6 Agree on the timing for the meeting (approx. 20 minutes).
7 Run the meeting (audio- or video-record it if possible).
8 Give the students language and communication feedback.

*Follow-up*
(*See also* 'How to . . . write an output document', p. x.)

- Organize groups for writing task.
- Give a time limit for drafting the job advertisement.
- Give the students language and communication feedback on writing.

*Key vocabulary*
bulletin board
candidate
classified ad
competent
initiative
profile
reliable
shift – shift working – shift worker
supervision
to recruit – a recruit – channels of recruitment

## Strategy meeting 3

### Market research questionnaire

*Introduction*
This agenda is based around a strategic business issue. The meeting will decide how to tackle the issue and the participants will write a document after the meeting decisions have been taken.
The issue concerns the contents of a market research questionnaire and the writing task is to draft the questions.

*Lead-in*
Ask your students:

- the purpose of market research
- if they have been interviewed by market researchers
- if they have received market research questionnaires
- their view of the effectiveness of market research.

*Method*
(*See also* 'Stages of the activity – standard procedures', p. viii.)

1 After the lead-in discussion, look at the problem itself.
2 Ask your students to read through the issue.
3 Make sure they all fully understand the problem.
4 Assign roles (chairman, secretary).
5 Allow 2 minutes to prepare (*see* pp. viii–ix).
6 Agree on the timing for the meeting (approx. 20 minutes).
7 Run the meeting (audio- or video-record it if possible).
8 Give the students language and communication feedback.

*Follow-up*
(*See also* 'How to . . . write an output document', p. x.)

- Organize groups for writing task.
- Give a time limit for drafting the questionnaire.
- Give the students language and communication feedback on writing.

*Key vocabulary*
coupon
household
income – income bracket
professional status
profile
questionnaire
survey

*Teacher's notes*

## Strategy meeting 4

### Early retirement document

*Introduction*
This agenda is based around a strategic business issue. The meeting will decide how to tackle the issue and the participants will write a document after the meeting decisions have been taken.
The issue concerns early retirement and the writing task is to draft a letter outlining the benefits of early retirement.

*Lead-in*
Ask your students:

- about the normal retirement age
- if managers take early retirement and in what circumstances
- what is offered in an early retirement package
- the benefits and drawbacks of early retirement.

*Method*
(*See also* 'Stages of the activity – standard procedures', p. viii.)

1 After the lead-in discussion, look at the problem itself.
2 Ask your students to read through the issue.
3 Make sure they all fully understand the problem.
4 Assign roles (chairman, secretary).
5 Allow 2 minutes to prepare (*see* pp. viii–ix).
6 Agree on the timing for the meeting (approx. 20 minutes).
7 Run the meeting (audio- or video-record it if possible).
8 Give the students language and communication feedback.

*Follow-up*
(*See also* 'How to . . . write an output document', p. x.)

- Organize groups for writing task.
- Give a time limit for drafting the letter.
- Give the students language and communication feedback on writing.

*Key vocabulary*
'corporate treadmill'
expert – expertise
headcount
secure
to acquire – acquisition
to expand one's horizons
to make redundant
to retire – retirement – early retirement package

## Brainstorming 1

### Managing your time

*Introduction*
This meeting does not have an agenda. It is designed to encourage students to be creative in their ideas and also in terms of running the meeting.
The meeting should focus on improving time management.

*Lead-in*
Discuss brainstorming meetings. What are the best ways of handling them? How can you make them creative but organized?

*Method*
(*See also* 'Stages of the activity – standard procedures', p. viii.)

1 After the lead-in discussion, give the group 3 minutes to read through the situation.
2 Tell them to organize the meeting, i.e. chairman, timing, secretary, etc.
3 Run the meeting (a flip chart/board will be useful).
4 Give feedback.

*Follow-up*
(*See also* 'How to . . . write an output document', p. x.)
Minutes and a memo.

*Key vocabulary*
diary/calendar/schedule/planner
time:
    to run out of time
    to save time
    to spend time
    to waste time

*Teacher's notes*

## Brainstorming 2

### Management tools

*Introduction*

This meeting does not have an agenda. It is designed to encourage students to be creative in their ideas and also in terms of running the meeting.
The meeting should focus on finding new management tools.

*Lead-in*

Discuss brainstorming meetings. What are the best ways of handling them? How can you make them creative but organized?

*Method*

(*See also* 'Stages of the activity – standard procedures', p. viii.)

1 After the lead-in discussion, give the group 3 minutes to read through the situation.
2 Tell them to organize the meeting, i.e. chairman, timing, secretary, etc.
3 Run the meeting (a flip chart/board will be useful).
4 Give feedback.

*Follow-up*

(*See also* 'How to . . . write an output document', p. x.)
Minutes and the description of a new management tool

*Key vocabulary*

effectiveness – effective
efficiency – efficient
project – project management
team – team-building – team working
to delegate – delegation
to fail – failure
to succeed – success – successful
to thrive

## Brainstorming 3

### What's in a name

*Introduction*

This meeting is designed to encourage students to be creative in their ideas and also in terms of running the meeting.
The meeting should focus on brainstorming names for a new product.

*Lead-in*

Discuss brainstorming meetings. What are the best ways of handling them? How can you make them creative but organized?

*Method*

(*See also* 'Stages of the activity – standard procedures', p. viii.)

1 After the lead-in discussion, give the group 3 minutes to read through the situation.
2 Tell them to organize the meeting, i.e. chairman, timing, secretary, etc.
3 Run the meeting (a flip chart/board will be useful).
4 Give feedback.

*Follow-up*

(*See also* 'How to . . . write an output document', p. x.)
Minutes

*Key vocabulary*

domestic market
mountain bike
socio-economic class
to launch
top end of the market
tourer

*Teacher's notes*

## Brainstorming 4

### A new logo

*Introduction*
This meeting does not have an agenda. It is designed to encourage students to be creative in their ideas and also in terms of running the meeting.
The meeting should focus on designing a new logo.

*Lead-in*
Discuss brainstorming meetings. What are the best ways of handling them? How can you make them creative but organized?

*Method*
(*See also* 'Stages of the activity – standard procedures', p. viii.)
1. After the lead-in discussion, give the group 3 minutes to read through the situation.
2. Tell them to organize the meeting, i.e. chairman, timing, secretary, etc.
3. Run the meeting (a flip chart/board will be useful).
4. Give feedback.

*Follow-up*
(*See also* 'How to . . . write an output document', p. x.)
Minutes and a memo.

*Key vocabulary*
artwork
classy
colour
design
dramatic
graphics
logo design
logotype
shading
typeface

## Brainstorming 5

### The company excursion

*Introduction*
This meeting does not have an agenda. It is designed to encourage students to be creative in their ideas and also in terms of running the meeting.
The meeting centres on a decision over a company excursion.

*Lead-in*
Discuss brainstorming meetings. What are the best ways of handling them? How can you make them creative but organized?

*Method*
(*See also* 'Stages of the activity – standard procedures', p. viii.)
1. After the lead-in discussion, give the group 3 minutes to read through the situation.
2. Tell them to organize the meeting, i.e. chairman, timing, secretary, etc.
3. Run the meeting (a flip chart/board will be useful).
4. Give feedback.

*Follow-up*
(*See also* 'How to . . . write an output document', p. x.)
Minutes and a memo.

*Key vocabulary*
funfair
leisure complex
open roof bus
outdoor pursuits:
    canoeing
    orienteering
    rock climbing
    white-water rafting

## The Agendas

# Material for photocopying

# CASE STUDY 1

## Company language

**ISSUE**

'English is the key to success and we must all improve.' These were the words of the new Chief Executive Officer (CEO), brought in two years ago to turn PCCorp around. PCCorp, a manufacturer of personal computers, had a brief spell of success in the eighties, but only just survived into the nineties. Two years ago, it was bought by the international giant, ITCorp. A new senior management team was brought in and they introduced new management practices with a major emphasis on internationalization.

The message about learning English has not been well received throughout PCCorp in Rotaronga. Many people feel that the language is moving into too many areas. Rotarongan youth seem to be very influenced by British and American culture, and young people use English words for special effect. This growing domination of English has led some politicians to suggest (in private) that the Rotarongan language can only be preserved by limiting the introduction of new words from English.

The CEO's words have received a mixed response at PCCorp. The meeting has been called for the management committee to discuss what to do about the CEO's recommendation.

**AGENDA**

1 The role of English in the business world
2 Cultural implications
3 SWOT (Strengths Weaknesses Opportunities Threats) analysis at PCCorp
4 Training aspects

*Notes to the agenda*

1 The Managing Director will present the corporate view.
2 The Human Resources Director will present some local views.
3 The Marketing Manager will present the SWOT analysis.
4 The Training Manager will outline plans for training.
5 The Workers' Representative will present the views from the shop-floor.
6 The Admin (Administration) Manager will outline the current dilemma about documentation.
7 The meeting will take a decision about the future role of English in the company and any necessary steps to implement that decision.

# Case Study 1

## Continued...

**ROLES**

### Managing Director

After a number of years on foreign assignments for ITCorp, you have come back to Rotaronga to head the PCCorp operation. You know the necessity of good English language skills. Having been trained at Harvard, you speak English and Rotarongan (as well as a number of other languages). You are concerned about the influence that English is having in Rotarongan society. You would like to see English as the external company language, but want to keep Rotarongan in place as the company's internal language.

### Human Resources Director

You joined PCCorp as a young graduate 20 years ago and have climbed the company hierarchy. In the last ten years, during PCCorp's financial troubles, you prevented widespread protests within the company, as wages and salaries were cut, emphasizing the role that PCCorp plays in the local community. You support an independent PCCorp. However, the recent takeover by ITCorp has changed the character of the company. You believe that the Anglicization of PCCorp is just another sell-out and will lead to the disappearance of the company very soon.

### Marketing Manager

To survive, PCCorp must sell into the local markets, which include neighbouring countries, where English is already widely spoken. Rotaronga has good ties with these countries and you can tap into established networks to develop the company's business. Without the local markets, PCCorp doesn't have a future and is likely to be closed down once the domestic market has been exploited. For PCCorp to survive, all your sales force need to be trained in English – and sooner rather than later.

### Training Manager

You have been charged with identifying potential suppliers of English language training. There are a number of local suppliers, who can provide basic language training. However, other larger companies tend to send their middle and senior management on training courses either in the US or in the UK. This is expensive and you favour using the local companies as this will keep the money in the local economy. However, you are aware of the poor feedback that the local providers have received.

### Workers' Representative

The shop-floor workers have faced great changes in working practices since the takeover by ITCorp. This has caused a degree of bad feeling. The workers are especially annoyed that a lot of documentation is now printed in English, when it could be translated into Rotarongan. It would cause fewer mistakes and would be less expensive than providing language support through training. The workers are not linguists and should not be expected to be competent in English.

### Admin (Administration) Manager

Having all the documentation in English is extremely useful, as it means that there is only one standard. Although it is not your native language, it would make your life and the life of your team easier.

# CASE STUDY 2

## Competition

**ISSUE**

*Five years ago your company employed a young computer expert, Geoff Peters. He has worked in the customer service department for the last two years. Essentially he supports a number of key customers doing maintenance and trouble-shooting work. Three months ago he suddenly left the company and he is now working for several of your customers, providing service as an independent computer consultant. His employment contract had a competition clause in it forbidding him from working for any customers for a two-year period after leaving. The meeting has been called to discuss this case and also to see whether any lesson can be learned for the future.*

**AGENDA**

1. Geoff Peters: report and discussion.
2. Competition clause
3. Legal action
4. Employment contracts

*Notes to the agenda*

1. *Geoff Peters: report and discussion.*
   The Personnel Manager will report on the case and then there will be a chance to discuss why Geoff left the company.
2. *Competition clause*
   The Legal Affairs Manager will clarify the exact meaning of the competition clause and the implications.
3. *Legal action*
   The meeting will decide whether to take Geoff Peters to court for breach of contract.
4. *Employment contracts*
   Finally a decision on whether the competition clause needs to be changed.

# Case Study 2

## Continued . . .

**ROLES**

*General Manager (Chair)*

You have an open mind on this case. On the one hand you can see that Geoff has broken his contract but on the other, you feel that it is a competitive market and your company has to face this sort of risk. Maybe the company should have worked harder to ensure that Geoff stayed with them.

*Personnel Manager*

You were on the interview panel which originally recruited Geoff. You feel he has been very well treated with a good salary, bonuses, training opportunities etc. You think he got greedy and decided to cut the company out. You think that he discussed leaving your company with key customers in order to negotiate contracts direct with them. You feel that he has broken his contract and must be taken to court. The clause in the contract should be made even tighter to ensure that employees do not dare to break it.

*Legal Affairs Manager*

The clause states: 'The employee is forbidden from soliciting and accepting business from any existing customer of the company for a two-year period following his or her resignation from the company.'

You feel the clause is quite clear, although Geoff's lawyer might argue that the customers were no longer 'existing' since they had decided to work with Geoff. You are unsure about taking Geoff to court. The company would probably win the case but at a high cost – both financially and to goodwill with customers. You feel this sort of thing is very difficult to legislate against and are not in favour of changing the clause.

*Customer Services Manager*

You were Geoff's boss for the last two years. He was very good at his job and all the customers he worked with were very happy with the service he gave them. You are not surprised that he has left. You feel your company does not pay computer experts enough (you think their salaries should be nearly doubled). These sort of people are very difficult to find and to keep. You don't think he should be taken to court. You think he should be offered a better deal in order to come back to the company.

*Sales Manager*

You are extremely upset about losing Geoff since he had built up a very good relationship with several key customers. You don't know what is the best next step. You would like to persuade Geoff to return to the company. On the other hand, you feel he has been disloyal. You don't agree that he wasn't paid enough. He was paid more than your sales people and they have to work extremely hard.

*Finance Manager*

You think he should be taken to court. He has broken his contract and an example must be made; otherwise other employees may think they can do the same. You also think the employment contract needs to be made much tighter.

# CASE STUDY 3

## Corruption

**ISSUE**

Your company has been accused of winning a number of large contracts by paying bribes to local council planning officers. No bribes have been paid but it is true that the company has developed a close relationship with some planning officers. The newspapers have printed photographs of senior managers dining with the Chief Planning Officer and some of his staff.

This meeting has been called to discuss the bad press you have received and how you can counteract it.

**AGENDA**

1. **Update on press reports**
2. **Relationships with council**
3. **New policy**
4. **Action plan**

*Notes to the agenda*

1. *Update on press reports*
   The Marketing Manager will update the meeting on any further reports.
2. *Relationships with council*
   A discussion about whether relationships are too close.
3. *New policy*
   Agreement of new guidelines on handling customers
4. *Action plan*
   Implementation of guidelines and response to press reports

# Case Study 3

*Continued...*

## ROLES

### Managing Director

You are aware that much of the company's success over the last five years has been due to the marketing department's policy of developing client relations. Your company has no written policy about 'wining and dining' clients but you feel it's part of everyday business and acceptable as long as it is not abused. You want the press story about bribes to be immediately contradicted and any further damage to the image of the company limited.

### Marketing Manager

During the last five years you have worked hard to maintain and develop clients. You have never bribed anybody but you have taken planning officers out to restaurants. You now realize that this may have been unwise. A local journalist has started writing stories about corruption in business. He says that it is very difficult for small companies to win contracts because companies like yours have a strong influence over council decisions. You feel the journalist has gone too far and your company should take his paper to court for libel.

### Public Relations Officer

Your job is to deal with the press. You feel taking legal action would be a mistake. You would prefer to start a campaign emphasizing the positive contribution your company makes to the community.

### Personnel Manager

You are concerned about how the bad image will affect motivation amongst the employees of the company. On the other hand, you think the Marketing Manager has done a good job in increasing the business over the last five years. This has had a very positive effect on recruitment and staff morale.

### Legal Advisor

You work in the legal department. The newspaper does not have real evidence of any bribes so you feel you would win the case if you took the paper to court. However, this would be a slow and expensive process and would keep the company in the headlines for a long time. You would prefer not to go to court.

### Sales Manager

You think your colleague in marketing has done a very good job and you know the talk of bribes is untrue. You think taking clients out to dinner is absolutely normal. You think there is no need for any guidelines and the newspaper should be sued for libel.

# CASE STUDY 4

## Dress

**ISSUE**

*Your company has an unwritten dress policy. Male employees are expected to wear ties and jackets; female employees smart dresses, skirts or trousers. Some staff employed in the information technology (IT) department have started to wear much more casual clothes, such as jeans, T-shirts, trainers etc. This is causing some bad feeling in the company as other staff, for example in sales, accounts and marketing, continue to wear formal clothes.*

*This meeting has been called to decide whether the dress code should be enforced.*

**AGENDA**

1. **Dress policy**
2. **IT department 'dress policy'**
3. **Enforcing the policy?**

*Notes to the agenda*

1. *Dress policy*

    The Administration Manager will outline the reasons for having a dress code. Others will give their opinions.

2. *IT department 'dress policy'*

    The Information Technology Manager will explain why he or she does not enforce the code. Others will state their points of view.

3. *Enforcing the policy?*

    A decision will be made as to whether the IT department should be brought into line with the rest of the company.

# Case Study 4

## Continued . . .

### ROLES

#### Administration Manager (Chair)

The company has a dress code because you are in a business where your customers tend to dress formally. Therefore, to respect their habits, you feel all staff should follow the code. It is true that some employees, like those in the information technology (IT) department, do not come into contact with customers. However, you feel it is divisive for one department to be treated differently.

#### Information Technology Manager

You have allowed dress in your department to become more informal. You feel that your department does a very good job for the company, servicing and supporting all the information technology needs; many of the staff work much longer hours than they are paid for. It is therefore very important to create a relaxed and tolerant working environment. Allowing the staff freedom to dress as they want makes them more motivated and prepared to put in long hours. In addition your staff have no contact with customers.

#### Sales Manager

You have been annoyed to see IT staff wandering around the building in jeans and T-shirts, while all your staff are smartly dressed. You think the tone of the company is being lowered. There is a dress code and it should be enforced.

#### Finance Manager

Although your staff do not usually come into contact with customers, you insist that they are always smartly dressed. You believe smart dress reflects well on the job and the company as a whole. You think the Information Technology Manager has made a big mistake in allowing his staff so much freedom. You admit that the information technology department does a very good job.

#### Marketing Manager

You think the way people dress is strongly associated with the image of the company. All your staff dress quite formally. You have some sympathy with the IT staff as their job is quite stressful and carried out entirely inside the company. You think the dress code should be relaxed – for example, no need for ties and jackets, but not jeans and T-shirts.

# CASE STUDY 5

## The environment

**ISSUE**

Your company is running out of space and needs to build an extension to accommodate additional staff. The only space available is presently occupied by a small lake. When the weather is good staff sit out by the lake at lunch-times. A small group takes a special interest in the lake and its environment. They have stocked it with fish and have encouraged wildlife to use the lake as its habitat. When plans were announced to build the extension, around 50 per cent of the staff were strongly against the plan on environmental grounds. The other 50 per cent are in favour of the extension, because it will mean more jobs.

The meeting has been called for the management committee to discuss the issues and decide how to handle them.

An agenda has been agreed.

**AGENDA**

1. Environmental implications
2. Financial implications
3. Employment
4. Alternative sites
5. Decision and communication to staff

*Notes to the agenda*

1. *Environmental implications*

   The spokesperson of the 'Save our Lake' group will present the arguments against building the extension. This should be followed by discussion

2. *Financial implications*

   The Finance Manager will present the costings for the extension and any alternatives

3. *Employment*

   Human Resources Manager will outline the plans for recruitment once the extension is completed.

4. *Alternative sites*

   The Managing Director will present a summary of the alternative sites which have been considered.

5. *Decision and communication to staff*

   Following the presentation and discussion above, a decision will be made and action decided about how to communicate to the employees.

# Case Study 5

## Continued . . .

### ROLES

#### Managing Director

You feel there is no alternative to building the extension on the site of the lake. It is the cheapest and most efficient solution. There are alternative sites but it would mean a split site and you think this would be very inefficient. The only other option is to relocate the whole company. There are some good sites in other regions and grants to support a move. However, you feel this decision would be very unpopular with all the employees.

#### Spokesperson (Save our Lake)

Five years ago you and three colleagues formed a group to look after the lake. It is now a beautiful site, flourishing with trees and flowers, and there are fish, ducks and even a pair of swans. You feel such sites are very rare, especially in an industrial area. The company has to find an alternative to filling in the lake.

#### Finance Manager

The cost of building the extension will be £1,550,000. This compares with £850,000 if you buy a purpose-built block to house new staff in the area. The estimated additional management and running costs from managing two sites are reckoned to be £350,000 a year. The cheapest option is to move to a new purpose-built site in the south-west of the country for under £1 million. There would be a lot of additional costs from relocation, and transport costs for your products would increase substantially.

#### Human Resources Manager

Although you like the lake, you feel the new extension must go ahead. It will mean a single site employing 1,400 people within two years (present headcount: 850 employees). This will be good news for the community and will increase production capacity by 75 per cent. You previously worked for a company with several sites and are strongly against this solution. You also don't think a total relocation is a realistic solution.

#### Production Manager

The new extension will enable you to increase capacity by 75 per cent over two years. The work environment will improve as well. However, you are sympathetic to the *Save our Lake* group. You like to spend your lunch-times by the lake and sometimes you come fishing in the evenings. You feel a split site is possible although not ideal. You could use the other site for material and finished product storage, thus freeing more space in the existing site to increase capacity. You think the lake and its environment are more important than higher profits.

#### Marketing Manager

You like the lake a lot. You also feel it's very good for the company's image in the local community. You agree with the Production Manager that the company should make some sacrifices to save the habitat around and in the lake.

# CASE STUDY 6

## Equal opportunities

**ISSUE**

BritPit is one of the newly privatized underground coal mines. The company uses powerful equipment to extract the coal, a sophisticated conveyor belt to transport the coal, and reliable support systems to protect the miners from the coal above.

Mining has become much safer in recent years due to much stricter safety legislation, though accidents still occur. Most of these are related to human error. It is therefore essential that there be extensive training of all people who work in mines.

BritPit employs 300 people at the coalface, in administration and in management. The coal-mining industry has traditionally been a male-dominated world – both in terms of workers and in terms of management. In an effort to move with the times, BritPit is considering taking on a number of women throughout the company. A meeting has been called to discuss in what areas women should or could be employed.

**AGENDA**

1. The work environment in coal mining
2. Modern times
3. The case for women in the workforce

*Notes to the agenda*

1. The Production Director will present the work environment in the mine.
2. The Human Resources Manager will present the needs of the company.
3. The Workers' Representative will outline conditions in the pit.
4. The Women's Lobby (or their representatives) will present their case.
5. The Health and Safety Manager will present health and safety aspects.
6. The Managing Director will review the case.
7. The meeting will draw up a policy document on the employment of women at BritPit.

# Case Study 6

*Continued . . .*

## ROLES

### Production Director

Although the mining industry is traditionally a man's world, you believe that the attitudes that this promotes are unhealthy. You have worked in a number of heavy industries and believe that women can be well integrated into the workforce. The mining industry requires a range of skills. Clearly those jobs which need physical strength will best be carried out by men. However, new technology has decreased the reliance on physical strength and many new jobs depend on teamwork and communication skills – areas where you believe that a mixed workforce can excel.

### Human Resources Manager

BritPit is located in a traditional mining area from which the company recruits all grades of workers and administrative staff. Managers, however, live in nearby small towns or villages. Miners are not badly paid, well above the national average for workers. In addition, overtime payments boost the wage packets still further. The privatization of BritPit has brought a lot of local resentment, especially as many jobs have been lost. In fact you estimate that 40 per cent of local families are now without a wage-earner. You believe that, by jobsharing, initially in the administrative area and later in the pit area, more jobs can be created. You believe that you can attract many women to jobsharing or part-time working in the administrative area and you would like to integrate women into the pit workforce, though you are not sure how.

### Workers' Representative

Working in a pit is hot, smelly and dangerous. It is certainly not women's work. In fact you believe that the whole coal-mining industry should stay firmly a male preserve.

### Women's Lobby

You have been members of a national group promoting the role of women in business and industry. You findings show that:

- women are more flexible than men in terms of part-time and jobshare working
- management teams which include women operate more effectively
- women who have joined the workforce in many traditional industries have helped to improve productivity.

You would like your ideas to be accepted in coal-mining because you believe that women can make a positive contribution in all areas of the workforce as well as management.

### Health and Safety Manager

You have worked for many years in the coal-mining industry and have worked your way up from being a miner. In your view coal mines are both dangerous and unhealthy, though conditions have improved in recent years. Although you accept that women could work in a mine, you don't believe that it is the right environment.

### Managing Director (MD)

You have been brought in to reorganize BritPit and improve profitability. You are sceptical about the role of women, but are prepared to listen to the arguments for and against.

# CASE STUDY 7

## Food terrorism

**ISSUE**

*SuperCo is a chain of 250 supermarkets selling food and drink through its nationwide stores. It stocks many of its own brands, but also buys in well-known products. After a bruising price war with FoodCo, SuperCo has just registered a 15 per cent increase in takings. FoodCo accused SuperCo of selling products at a loss in order to attract customers, but SuperCo denies this allegation.*

*Yesterday evening, the Managing Director of SuperCo received an anonymous phone call from an animal activist group saying that the company's pâté de foie gras (duck's liver pâté), produced by an external supplier, had been mixed with rat poison. Two years ago, the supermarket received a similar phone call saying that the baby food in its stores had also been poisoned. The products were immediately removed from all the shelves but no evidence of any poison was found. This news was leaked to the press and resulted in a panic among many of SuperCo's customers. The result was a downturn in business that SuperCo's current discount campaign was intended to change.*

*An urgent meeting has been called to decide what action to take.*

**AGENDA**

1. Background to the present problem
2. Details of production
3. Action plan
4. Future implications

*Notes to the agenda*

   *The SuperCo team*
   1. SuperCo's Purchasing Director will bring the meeting up-to-date on the former scare and the present situation.
   2. The Public Relations Manager will outline the media implications.
   3. The Customer Services Manager will outline the options.

   *The supplier team*
   4. The Production Director will explain relevant details of the production process.
   5. The Sales Director will look at the sales implications.
   6. The Quality Manager will focus on the quality procedures.

   *Conclusion*
   7. The members of the meeting will decide:
      a) what steps are to be taken
      b) how these steps are to be taken
      c) by whom these steps should be taken.

# Case Study 7

## Continued . . .

**ROLES**

### SuperCo's Purchasing Director

(First you will need to go over the details of the case from the briefing notes.)
In the last scare you ordered the immediate withdrawal of all baby food products from the shelves. The result was disastrous. The media got hold of the story and SuperCo was targeted by a whole range of consumer interest groups, mostly hostile to the company. This time you intend to be more balanced. The customers come first, but you must protect the company's interests. You would like to be persuaded that this is only a false alarm.

### SuperCo's Public Relations Manager

Last time you felt that you put on a good show for the cameras and the press. Your reassuring ways made a big impression and helped to minimize the impact of the scare. The company had done the right thing by withdrawing the products. That certainly made your life easier. You feel that the company should do the same this time. In fact, you are quite looking forward to the media attention.

### SuperCo's Customer Services Manager

You have sent 100 sample jars of pâté de foie gras from 15 local supermarkets to laboratories for examination. The results have shown that the jars have not been opened and the pâté de foie gras has not been contaminated
   From your point of view, the company has the following three options:

1  to withdraw the pâté de foie gras without further testing
2  to carry out tests on samples from all supermarkets and make a decision in the evening
3  to ignore the warning as a hoax.

Of course, you have only tested a small sample from a small proportion of the chain, but you feel this is another false alarm.

### Production Director

You receive the pâté de foie gras from abroad, already packaged. Your main job is to label it for the final customer. You have 10 key customers for this product. You had a warning call that your products would be targeted by an animal activist group, but that was more than 3 years ago, before SuperCo became a customer. You always believed it was a hoax. Maybe now you should take it more seriously. Should you contact your customers or would that would simply raise the alarm?

### Sales Director

Sales for pâté de foie gras are booming. Customers are developing a taste for more exotic products and you are delighted with the results. The industry is full of scare stories about activists. You feel that this is simply another hoax.

### Quality Manager

You oversee the quality procedures during manufacture abroad. You have heard on the grapevine about animal activists, but you have nothing which proves that they have ever taken action to poison the producer's pâté de foie gras.

# CASE STUDY 8

## Going international

**ISSUE**

*Streamline is a management consultancy (six partners and 50 associates) offering services in rationalizing and streamlining small- and medium-size enterprises (SMEs). In the nineties, their services were in great demand as companies made efforts to increase productivity and reduce costs. To keep up with demand for their services, Streamline grew considerably in the nineties. However, the movement towards downsizing is coming to an end, as many companies have now contracted to their optimum (minimum) size. One of the options for Streamline is to find new markets for their services. As many neighbouring countries are about to face up to the challenge of rationalization, Streamline are in an excellent position to offer their consultancy services abroad. However, they have no experience of doing business abroad. How does a small consultancy go international?*

**AGENDA**

    1  The requirements of going international

    2  The implications of going international

*Notes to the agenda*

*The six partners:*

1. offer their views on going international
2. discuss the steps to be taken to go international
3. decide which steps should be taken.

# Case Study 8

## Continued . . .

## ROLES

### Partner 1

You are committed to going international. You believe that you will find a market for your services. Your main concern is that you will have contact with foreigners. Although you don't like to admit it, your strong feelings of nationalism are sometimes tinged with xenophobia. You think that the partners would be unhappy if you voiced your views, so you have always kept them to yourself.

### Partner 2

You have mixed feelings about going international. You see all countries as different and hard to understand. You think that Streamline could sell its services in some countries, but you are concerned that it might require more effort than you are prepared to commit. You are not prepared to commit money, though, to setting up local offices.

You feel a thorough investigation should be made of possible target markets so that a balanced evaluation can be made of the risks and threats.

### Partner 3

Going international would be a real personal and professional challenge, and certainly shouldn't be underestimated. You would like to see Streamline offices in all the region's major capitals. You would derive great satisfaction from setting them up and paying regular visits. Local differences don't worry you. The Streamline formula for rationalizing companies should work anywhere – as long as it is in the right hands. And those hands should be Streamline hands.

### Partner 4

You believe that expansion of Streamline will create new job and career opportunities. You like the idea of working with local partners since this would be less of a financial risk than setting up your own office. You have been contacted by a number of foreign consultancies interested in local arrangements. You think that this type of association could be a very attractive proposition.

### Partner 5

You believe that Streamline can expand abroad, but that it will be difficult to manage the projects. Having worked abroad you realize that success depends on professional expertise, and on local knowledge and cultural sensitivity. Many small companies have oversimplified the business calculations and underestimated the cultural differences. Working abroad is much more difficult than working at home. You feel that the other partners don't recognize the factors involved.

### Partner 6

Your earlier experience of working in an organization with foreign partners has made you suspicious. On that occasion, poor communication between the offices finally led to breakup of the partnership and the subsequent loss of clients. You could be persuaded, but you need to be convinced that the partners understand the importance of building relationships and trust through open communication.

# CASE STUDY 9

## Information flow

**ISSUE**

*Of all the activities that managers engage in, communication is probably the most important. It maintains personal relationships and it transmits messages. There can be too much communication, as some of the six partners of FinServe, a financial services company feel. At present they have:*

- *a monthly business meeting*
- *a monthly finance meeting – forecasting and reviewing*
- *a monthly marketing meeting – overview of new developments in the market place*
- *a monthly quality meeting – everything from premises to business cards*
- *a quarterly personnel meeting – current staffing needs*
- *a half-yearly review meeting.*

*As the partners spend a lot of time out of the office with clients, these meetings are usually held in the evenings (after 18.00) and, in fact, it is rare for all the partners to be present at all the meetings. The meetings are prepared, with an agenda, a chairperson and follow-up minutes which are circulated to the partners.*

*A meeting has been called to evaluate the effectiveness of the present system and to see whether a better arrangement can be made.*

**AGENDA**

1. The purposes of the meetings
2. Other possible arrangements
3. Follow-up plans for information

*Notes to the agenda*

*The six partners:*
1. offer their views on the effectiveness of the present arrangements
2. discuss alternative arrangements
3. decide what steps should be taken and who should take them.

# Case Study 9

## Continued . . .

**ROLES**

*Partner 1*

You believe that the present system works well. The meetings are the only forum in which to discuss matters affecting the business. You feel that the marketing and finance meetings are often seen as low priority.

*Partner 2*

You believe meetings take up too much time. Some of the regular meetings last two hours. You believe that meetings could be completed in half that time. You would like the partners to agree on better time-keeping during the meetings with fewer interruptions and diversions. Your ideal is the financial meeting, which you usually chair. Here you present the figures for the last period, then you present the forecasts for the next period. The meeting is usually over within half an hour.

*Partner 3*

The quality meeting could be handled by two or three of the partners. Your view is that these topics should be included in the business meeting agenda so that a decision could be made as to who would take them over. The financial meeting isn't really a meeting at all. These figures could easily be printed out and circulated. Any questions could then be discussed at the business meeting.

*Partner 4*

You feel that the present arrangements are rather cumbersome. With your young family, the demands of late evening work are beginning to cause stress. You want the meetings to be held in the mornings. In any case, that's your best time. Every week there are two to three pages of minutes. This information could be circulated in some electronic form.

*Partner 5*

You believe that the meetings could be streamlined if more information was made available in advance. If the information for the finance meeting was circulated in advance, then the meeting might be more productive. At present, the partners spend most of the meeting listening to an explanation of the figures. There are rarely any comments or questions.

*Partner 6*

You dislike the way the meetings are managed. You believe that there are different types of meetings for different purposes: discussion meetings, decision-making meetings, briefing meetings, and brainstorming meetings. You would like to discuss the appropriateness of these meeting types for the business of the partnership. You believe that:

- the monthly business meeting should be a decision-making meeting
- the monthly finance meeting should be a briefing meeting
- the monthly marketing meeting should be a brainstorming meeting
- the monthly quality meeting should be a discussion meeting
- the quarterly personnel meeting should be a briefing meeting
- the half-yearly review meeting should be a discussion meeting.

# CASE STUDY 10

## International assignments

**ISSUE**

Your company has broken into a number of foreign markets during the last five years and you have had to send project managers, engineers and technicians to support local people in these markets. These assignments have lasted from 2 weeks to 2 years. These postings have begun to cause real unhappiness amongst the staff involved. Some are refusing to be sent abroad again, others are demanding much higher allowances for working abroad. It is time for you to formulate a policy for staff working overseas.

**AGENDA**

1. The problem
2. Duration of assignments
3. Compensation for foreign assignments
4. Family support
5. International training
6. Career development
7. Action plan

*Notes to the agenda*

1. *The problem*
   The chairperson will outline the scope of the problem.
2. *Duration of assignments*
   The Senior Project Manager will talk about the nature of the assignments. Discussion of duration.
3. *Compensation for foreign assignments*
   The Personnel Manager will lead a discussion of compensation rates.
4. *Family support*
   Discussion of whether assignments should be accompanied or not.
5. *International training*
   The Training Manager will introduce this item.
6. *Career development*
   The Human Resources Manager will introduce the possible ways of developing international career paths.
7. *Action plan*
   Conclusions from the meeting and agreeing the next steps to take.

# Case Study 10

## Continued . . .

**ROLES**

### The Chairperson

During the last five years, 55 staff have been sent abroad, most of them on short assignments, but around 15 engineers have been sent on longer assignments (from 3 months – 2 years). They have gone to countries where conditions are hard. You have compensated staff but there have been complaints and it is now difficult to find people willing to go overseas. This is a major problem since 25 per cent of your turnover is abroad and it is increasing.

### Senior Project Manager

You have been on two assignments of 6 months and 15 months. Both were unaccompanied. You can understand why young engineers are not very keen, especially if they have families. You think that assignments from 3–6 months should be paid double the usual salary rates. Assignments of over 6 months should be accompanied by families. The company must treat these engineers well if it wants to persuade them to work abroad.

### Personnel Manager

Engineers are paid their salary plus an allowance of 25 per cent extra for every working day spent abroad. You feel this is quite generous, as the money is tax free and living expenses are covered by the company separately. Long assignments are very tough and not really for families. The company could introduce a range of benefits:

- 0–3 months: 5 per cent extra salary
- 3–6 months: 25 per cent extra salary
- 6–24 months: 35 per cent extra salary

There will be no overall increase in the salary bill but it will compensate for long assignments more generously.

### Training Manager

You do not offer any special training for work overseas. You now think a number of options could be offered: language training, cross-cultural briefing, and interpersonal training support for hardship posts. These courses could be offered to both staff and spouses, where the assignment is going to be accompanied.

### Human Resources Manager

You want to offer fast-track promotion for those staff who are prepared to work overseas. You would like to develop an International Project Management Group which would administer overseas contracts and the staff working on them. Staff who gain international experience will be ear-marked for senior management positions early in their careers.

### Project Manager

You have been on a number of assignments. You feel pay should be double for work abroad, except for very short contracts (up to 4 weeks). You don't feel it is a good idea for the staff to be accompanied by their partners. You think the company should pay for return air fares every 3 months, so that staff can stay in touch with their families, and holiday entitlement should be doubled.

# CASE STUDY 11

## International joint venture

**ISSUE**

Your company has set up a joint venture with a local company in a new market. The aim of this joint venture is to enter a new market with the benefit of local knowledge. The local company is small, just the owner and five employees. Your company employs 2,400 staff throughout the world.

The main terms of the joint venture are that you will invest $25,000 in the first year for marketing and distribution. You will earn 5 per cent of the expected turnover of $200,000 in the first year; in the second year, you will invest a further $15,000 and take 5 per cent of an expected turnover of $350,000. In the third year, you will invest just $10,000 for a 5 per cent return on forecasted turnover of $500,000. All conditions are subject to revision on an annual basis dependent on targets being achieved and the contract respected.

You are midway through the first year and turnover is running well below target (just $60,000 in 6 months). Your investment has already been made. Relations with your foreign partner are not good. He does not speak your language, you don't speak his. He says there have been a lot of unforeseen problems, you feel you don't have enough control. You have asked for a meeting next month.

This meeting has been called to discuss the options open to you to try and get the joint venture back on track.

**AGENDA**

1. Market report
2. Financial report
3. Options:

    a) recruitment of a local employee to oversee the joint venture

    b) more regular reporting

    c) plan to abandon joint venture at end of first year.

4. Action plan

*Notes to the agenda*

1. *Market report*
    The Marketing Manager will report on the first 6 months of operation
2. *Financial report*
    The Finance Manager will report on the figures.
3. *Options*
    The meeting will discuss all the options.
4. *Action plan*
    An agenda for the meeting with the local partner will be finalized.

# Case Study 11

## Continued . . .

**ROLES**

### Managing Director

This joint venture was your idea and you feel it much too early to talk about pulling out. You want to go to the meeting next month in a positive frame of mind.

### Marketing Manager

You feel the joint venture is not working. You would be better off with direct control. In the first 6 months, the local company has gained a lot of customers (more than expected) but, in many cases, has failed to supply them. As a result, billing is much lower than anticipated and there is a big danger of losing the goodwill that has already been created by the marketing effort financed by your $25,000. You think the answer is to start again at the end of the year, with a small sales office manned by your own people.

### Finance Manager

The first 6 months have been disappointing ($40,000 below budget). The sales have not come through and the cash flow is very poor. It seems the invoicing of the local partner is slow and inefficient. You favour taking a very strong line at next month's meeting. You think you should increase the per cent royalty of turnover and supply one of your team to oversee the finances of the joint venture locally.

### Area Sales Manager

You feel it is much too early to judge this joint venture. You think you should be offering more support to the local company without charging for it in the first year. All the market research shows that the market potential is enormous. The fact that they have already got a lot of customers underlines this. It seems it is more a problem of systems.

### Distribution Manager

You feel most of the problems are caused by poor distribution systems. You would like to go out next month and see their systems. You don't think the joint venture should be charged for your time and expenses. It needs to be given a chance to succeed.

# CASE STUDY 12

## Managing the project

**ISSUE**

*Advertising agencies are often viewed as nests of creativity, where artistic ideas are converted into business successes. AdItion, a six-person partnership plus associates and 20 employees) have been associated with many advertising campaigns for a wide range of products and services. Recently, however, they have begun to lose their edge. One project for a key client went over budget, another was delivered late. There have also been internal working problems in some of the project teams. The agency needs to reappraise its project management methods to ensure that creative endeavour is matched by organizational requirements. A meeting has been called to discuss the key aspects of project management.*

**AGENDA**

1. The need for creativity
2. Managing time
3. Managing people
4. Overall organization

*Notes to the agenda*

1. One of the partners will present the problems facing AdItion.
2. The Production Director will focus on the need for schedules and planning in the production process.
3. The Marketing Director will emphasize what clients expect from AdItion.
4. The Head of Design will outline the design concerns.
5. The Financial Director will present the financial implications.
6. The Team Leader will present problems of team-working.
7. The members of the meeting will decide on a set of guidelines for managing projects more effectively.

# Case Study 12

*Continued . . .*

## ROLES

### The Partner

AdItion has always been associated with innovation and creativity. Ideas count for everything. You believe that the strength of AdItion's position has been achieved through a mix of inspiration and hard work. Of course, you are well aware that deadlines have to be met, but you are convinced that without the creative force there would be no deadlines to meet.

### Production Director

Working in AdItion is a real challenge for you. There are no conventional production rules of planning and scheduling. This makes your job a real headache, since timetables are often not followed. Nobody has been too concerned about overruns (time), so you have taken a more flexible approach to production. As long as the company pays generously for overtime when there is a deadline to meet, you know that your workers will put in the extra hours.

### Marketing Director

You are dismayed by the recent results of the design teams. You have lost two key accounts because of delays in delivery. You have also had to give generous discounts to three clients because of the poor quality of the finished product. The company needs to become more rigorous in project planning and scheduling, and the terms of a project must be followed. If not, then it is no surprise when the client complains about late delivery or increased costs.

### Head of Design

Many of the ideas that you have recently been presented with really don't deserve to go beyond the drawing board. You feel that the pressure to be creative is becoming counter-productive. Also, teams are now in such a rush that they present poor ideas which can't be turned into design without a much fuller brief.

### Financial Director

The organic culture of AdItion doesn't fit with the requirements for financial planning and control. The successes of the early years allowed you to be rather more flexible than in more traditional companies. AdItion is not a conventional company, but the recent downturn in business is beginning to show in the books. The situation is also made worse by the discounts that you have given to clients because of late delivery and the enormous overtime bill for the production department.

### Team Leader

You work as a team leader and liaise with other team leaders. Certain teams are not gelling and you feel that the cause is the increased pressure on teams to produce results. This has led to a breakdown in the working relationship in teams. This has affected the results and you believe that more attention needs to be paid to the way that teams are formed for project work. Better balance and more focus on personal working styles will help teams to achieve more.

# CASE STUDY 13

## The millennium meeting

**ISSUE**

*Your company is a manufacturer of sportswear for schools and youth clubs. The main market for your products is the many schools and youth clubs throughout the country which offer sports, either as part of their timetable or as a leisure activity. At present you sponsor a number of national sports events and make charitable contributions to worthy causes.*

*Many initiatives are being prepared for the millennium. Your company has decided to make a sum of £20,000 available. No specific areas have been selected, but the overall idea is 'to make a lasting contribution with some visible outcome'. A millennium committee has therefore been set up with the specific task of deciding how the money should be spent.*

**AGENDA**

1. The purpose of the 'millennium fund'
2. The various options
3. Decision and follow-up action

*Notes to the agenda*

1. The Managing Director will present the purpose of the 'millennium fund'.
2. Each manager and representative will present their views on the best use of the fund.
3. The Managing Director will chair the meeting and lead it to a decision.

# Case Study 13

## Continued . . .

**ROLES**

### Managing Director

You believe that the fund is an ideal opportunity to make a contribution to sport in the community. It is important to re-establish sporting activities and values. The recent trend towards computer games has led to a fall in your company's turnover. As the millennium approaches, you believe that many parents are turning away from the 'computer games culture' and want their children to take up more active pursuits. You see your role in supporting these parents.

### Information Technology Manager

For the IT world, the millennium is a the time bomb which will bring computer systems to a halt as soon as their clocks reach 1 January 2000. Unable to differentiate between 2000 and 1900, systems will crash, causing untold chaos. You would like the money to be invested in a project, bringing together companies in the sportswear sector, to solve this problem. *Cost: £15,000*

### Marketing Director

You have always believed that well-targeted sponsorship will raise the company's profile. One of the most talked about events is 'the millennium run', a weekend run from the north to the south, ending up with a huge celebration in the capital. The company should provide sponsorship by making some of the shirts, with a prominent display of the company's logo. This will promote the company's products and make a clear statement about the role of sports and health for the country's youth. *Cost: £12,000*

### Personnel Manager

The moral decline in the younger generation seems to have left them without a clear direction in life. You are dismayed by the number of young people who sleep rough on the city's streets; even your contributions to the begging bowls meet with no response. You would like to see the company's millennium fund making a local contribution towards 'back to life' schemes. This would take young people off the streets, provide them with accommodation, training and find them jobs within the community – perhaps even within your company. *Cost: £20,000*

### Admin (Administration) Manager

Newtown, where your company is based, is a soulless place. The city's main landmark is MegaShop, a complex of shops, restaurants and leisure centres. It is an attractive venue to the under 40s, with loud music and bright lights. For the millennium, it is planning a local celebration, to be funded by local businesses. Many older people, however, avoid MegaShop. They say it is unfriendly, and there is nowhere to sit and rest, unless they go into one of the expensive restaurants. You could pay for the installation of some benches in the main concourse where people could rest. *Cost £5,000*

### Workers' Representative

Newtown needs more money for sport. The football team, of which you are the captain, is forever short of cash. Other local clubs face the same financial problems, and it is becoming more difficult to get young people to play sport. You would like to see the company promote sport more actively. For the millennium, you would like to see a special sports day, a mini-Olympics, with funds not only for the event itself, but also to support sports clubs with kit after the event. *Cost: sports day £10,000; sports clubs support £10,000.*

# CASE STUDY 14

## Multicultural project

**ISSUE**

*You are working on an international project with partners from two other countries.*

*The project has been delayed by a variety of problems. Relationships within the project group have deteriorated and it is becoming more and more difficult to work together. A meeting has been called for the project leaders from each country (two in each case) to get together and try to sort out the frustrations.*

**AGENDA**

1. Timing
2. Meetings
3. Reports
4. Hierarchy
5. Action plan

*Notes to the agenda*

1. *Timing*
   There seem to be different attitudes towards deadlines. This should be an opportunity to sort out the important milestones for the project.

2. *Meetings*
   Some people regard the project meetings as essential, others as a nuisance. Again an opportunity to reach common objectives about meetings and their purpose.

3. *Reports*
   Different approaches to report writing exist in the group. Some write extremely long and detailed project updates, others just a few lines. Some always write minutes of a meeting and circulate them, others don't.

4. *Hierarchy*
   There are supposed to be just two layers of hierarchy in this project: project leader and project member.

5. *Action plan*
   Following the discussion of the above points, decisions should be made about how to improve relationships in the project.

# Case Study 14

## Continued . . .

**ROLES**

*Country 1: (project leader and project member)*

*Timing*: Deadlines are absolutely vital and they must be kept to. For you, the project will be a failure if it doesn't come in on time.
*Meetings*: They are chaotic; they are not chaired very well and nobody takes minutes and they seem to be just an opportunity to discuss things. All the decisions seem to be taken outside rather than during meetings.
*Reports*: All the steps of the project need to be recorded in memos, agendas, minutes and project updates; you notice that some things are written down, others not. You always send written memos and never rely just on the telephone.
*Hierarchy:* Some project leaders behave as if they are in charge of the whole project. For you, there is no overall project manager, it is a team effort. You have noticed that some team members regard themselves as more important than others.

*Country 2: (project leader and project member)*

*Timing*: Deadlines are important but you must be flexible. If there are problems which cause delays then the milestones will have to be changed.
*Meetings:* They are OK, as they are an opportunity to discuss things and to stay in touch. You don't see why they have to be chaired rigorously. Everybody knows what they have to do.
*Reports:* There is too much writing inside the project and it wastes a lot of time. You don't understand why every meeting has to be minuted, you all go the meetings so why write extensive minutes. You don't see why memos have to be written either.
*Hierarchy:* Some project leaders behave as if they are in charge of the whole project. For you, there is no overall project manager, it is a team effort. You have noticed that some team members regard themselves as more important than others.

*Country 3: (project leader and project member)*

*Timing:* Deadlines have to be flexible. Country 1 is making things worse by being so stressed about time. If there is a slight delay, it is not too serious.
*Meetings:* Many of the meetings are a waste of time. Most of the problems can be sorted out over the phone or face to face between the three project leaders.
*Reports:* It is important to write regular project updates to keep people informed. You don't see why the meetings need long minutes or why you need to write memos.
*Hierarchy:* You are aware that you have been taking some initiatives on your own but you think this has been necessary. In fact, you think one of the project leaders should be appointed as overall project manager.

# CASE STUDY 15

## New technology

**ISSUE**

*Two years ago a new computer system was installed in your company to process orders and purchases, keep track of all financial transactions, analyze performance and provide management with up-to-the-minute information, and write letters and perform other administrative tasks.*

*Some of the applications work rather slowly and there are times when the system crashes and is out of action for a short period. From a recent survey, opinions about the system are mixed, ranging from satisfied to dissatisfied. Many of the senior managers never use their computers. They rely on their secretaries or assistants to print out information and these staff members use their computers all the time.*

*The meeting has been called for the management committee to discuss a proposal to upgrade the system in order to provide more facilities, faster (more powerful) computers, and greater reliability.*

*This will involve scrapping the present computer system and installing new machines and some new software.*

**AGENDA**

1. **Work implications**
2. **Technological aspects**
3. **Training aspects**
4. **Personnel implications**

*Notes to the agenda*

1. The Administration Manager will present admin's views.
2. The User Group Representative will present the results of the survey.
3. The Information Technology Manager will present the arguments for investing in a new system.
4. The Training Director will outline training requirements for the existing system, as well as for the new system.
5. The Human Resources Director will outline implications for jobs in the company.
6. The Managing Director will lead the discussion around the key areas.
7. The members of the meeting will decide what steps must be taken to use computers more effectively within the company.

# Case Study 15

## Continued . . .

**ROLES**

*Administration Manager*

You have mixed views about computers: when they work, they are extremely useful; when they don't they are a real barrier to efficiency. At present, the system works most of the time and the administrative and secretarial personnel can handle the technology. You are concerned about the disruption caused by the proposed upgrade and the demands of learning to manage a new system. You are also worried about the information technology department, whom you have found unresponsive and unhelpful.

*User Group Representative*

The results of the user survey breaks down as follows:

- Younger administrative and secretarial staff are happy with the technology and keen to move on to more powerful machines. These will make their lives easier and enable them to work more quickly and easily.
- Administrative and secretarial staff over 35 are generally satisfied with the present setup. They feel that the current machines work well and enable them to carry out their tasks efficiently.
- The majority of management are satisfied with the information they get. Speed of response is not really a concern.

*Information Technology Manager*

Your main problem is with keeping staff. The good technicians soon move on to better jobs and you are left with the average ones. Many of the call-out requests from users are not 'technical' problems, they are the result of insufficient training. Your job is to solve technical faults, not teach staff how to use the software. You feel the proposed upgrade could make the system more stable and cause less technical problems. You think that more training will be needed for the company to benefit from the investment.

*Training Manager*

The company doesn't spend enough on training and software training is a prime example. If the upgrade goes ahead then the company will need to arrange training courses for the new software; otherwise it will be a catastrophe.

*Human Resources Director*

You are committed to the introduction of new technology. It will help to improve the poor reputation that the company has in the job market-place. If you can make the company a technological leader in its field, it will help to attract better personnel, including administrative and secretarial staff, to the company.

*Managing Director*

You see the introduction of new technology as a way of streamlining the operations, leading to greater productivity and higher profits. When the last system was installed, there was minimal disruption to the company's operations. There is no reason why the same should not be true this time.

# CASE STUDY 16

## Outsourcing

**ISSUE**

*Mavis and Bill work as cleaners at Staybright, a small manufacturing company employing some 250 people. They are almost the longest serving members of staff, apart from the family owners, who now play a background role in the company's affairs. Since they joined the company, it has gone through many management changes. Managers have come and managers have gone and with them new styles of management.*

*The latest trend in management at Staybright is outsourcing, though Mavis and Bill don't really understand what's behind it. All they know is that they may lose their jobs.*

**AGENDA**

1. The case for outsourcing
   The MD
   The Finance Director

2. The case for Mavis and Bill
   Mavis/Bill
   The Workers' Representative

3. The needs of the company
   The Administration Manager
   The Personnel Manager

*Notes to the agenda*

1. The Managing Director will present the general case for outsourcing non-core functions at Staybright.
2. The Finance Director will illustrate the savings to the company by outsourcing the cleaning.
3. Mavis/Bill will present their position as loyal members of the workforce.
4. The Workers' Representative will present the effect on morale of making Mavis and Bill redundant.
5. The Administration Manager will present Staybright's needs in terms of cleaning.
6. The Personnel Manager will review the impact of outsourcing from the personnel point of view.
7. The meeting will decide whether to outsource the cleaning function and how to handle the case of Mavis and Bill.

# Case Study 16

## *Continued . . .*

### ROLES

#### *Managing Director*

You have been brought in to save Staybright. You have to reorganize the company's operations and improve its profitability. There are some areas where subcontracting offers the possibility of cost saving. In the manufacture of some components, the cost of replacing specialist equipment will be very high and, in the long run, uneconomical. However, you are aware that outsourcing has an adverse effect on labour relations, and Staybright has always had a good labour relations record.

#### *Finance Director*

Mavis and Bill are paid £200 a week each plus 11 per cent for employer's contributions. However, this bill is increased by expensive cleaning materials. Mavis and Bill are now in their late 50s and no longer provide the standard of cleaning that the company needs. As part of your brief to look at ways of cutting costs, you believe that an outside contractor could save about 30 per cent, especially if the shop-floor workers can be persuaded to do part of the end-of-shift cleaning themselves.

#### *Mavis/Bill*

You have been loyal members of the workforce for almost 40 years and are nearly part of the family. You expect to continue working for Staybright until retirement at 65. You have always had a good relationship with the owners, have hardly ever been off sick and have always kept the small factory and the offices clean. You have recently been told that your jobs may have to go in order to save the company.

#### *Workers' Representative*

You believe that outsourcing is a very bad move for Staybright. The company is part of the local community and draws its workforce from people living in the area. If Mavis and Bill lose their jobs, it will have a serious negative effect on the morale of the company. At a time when the company is in financial difficulty, you believe that everyone should pull together.

#### *Administration Manager*

Staybright needs new cleaners, and as this is your responsibility, you would like to see a new arrangement. Mavis and Bill have done a good job for many years, but with age, they are becoming less efficient. There have been numerous complaints about the standard of cleaning in the offices and in the workshop.

#### *Personnel Manager*

You have been with Staybright for 15 years and have seen its performance slip. The steady stream of managers, who have come, changed management policies and then moved on, has not helped. You think that companies thrive in an environment where employees feel that they have a stake in the company. At Staybright this used to be the case, but the recent trend towards rationalization and outsourcing have reduced company morale to an all-time low.

# CASE STUDY 17

## Pay versus benefits

**ISSUE**

In the early 1990s Systemtech was one of the leading Internet Service Providers. Started by two computer science graduates in a garage in Newtown, it quickly grew to be a multi-million pound business. Last year, after increasing complaints about the management of the business, the two founders sold out, though they still sit as advisory directors on the board. Today Systemtech (present headcount 250) is struggling to find new products for a more sophisticated market-place. The new management is also struggling to control the payroll. One method would be to reduce benefits, though this would certainly be met by opposition within the company.

These are the present benefits:

- a salary
- a performance-related bonus (up to 100 per cent of the salary)
- subsidized lunches
- annual health screening
- health club membership

In addition, directors and managers receive:

- company cars, paid petrol and free parking
- private medical insurance
- life assurance
- financial planning

**AGENDA**

1. **The benefits package at Systemtech**
2. **The payroll bill**
3. **Motivation aspects**
4. **Practical implications**

*Notes to the agenda*

1. The Managing Director will present the benefits package.
2. The Finance Director will present the savings target.
3. The Research and Development Director will present the advantages.
4. The Human Resources Manager will outline motivational aspects.
5. The Workers' Representative will outline the workers' view.
6. The Administration Manager will present key admin (administration) issues.
7. The meeting will decide on the elements of the future benefits package for Systemtech managers and employees.

# Case Study 17

## Continued . . .

**ROLES**

### Managing Director

If Systemtech is to survive, you need to change attitudes towards remuneration. You summarize the benefits. You believe that the company should only provide a salary and performance-related bonus.

### Finance Director

You need to save £300,000 from next year's payroll bill. Each benefit costs:

- a performance-related bonus (£500,000)
- subsidized lunches (£20,000)
- annual health screening (£5,000)
- health club membership (£18,000)
- company cars, paid petrol and free parking (£120,000)
- private medical insurance (£75,000)
- life assurance (£55,000)
- financial planning (£7,500)

You believe that performance-related bonus is a useful incentive, but that not everyone who receives the bonus deserves it. The other benefits should all be scrapped and basic salaries increased.

### R&D Director

Systemtech needs to attract the brightest young engineers. Many of them are now going to Australia. The only way that you can attract them and keep them is by offering a creative working environment and an excellent remuneration package. This must include a bonus system.

### Human Resources Manager

The more you offer, the more people want. It is much better to have a higher basic salary, and get rid of the unjust bonus system and all the other unnecessary benefits. You are convinced that these elements have only a short-term motivational value. What is important is the working environment and Systemtech should spend more on that.

### Workers' Representative

The workers generally like the benefits system. It helps to increase the basic salaries and wages, which have not changed for two years.

### Administration Manager

The benefits system involved a lot of work for you and your team, especially the health-related and insurance-related benefits. However, you would like to keep the benefits system, as you believe it provides motivation for company employees. You need one additional admin (administration) person to administer the different schemes at a cost of around £15,000 per year.

# CASE STUDY 18

## Quality

**ISSUE**

*You work for a small information technology (IT) services company. You are considering applying for ISO 9000 accreditation. Some of your competitors have this stamp of quality approval and it could help in winning new contracts. You have calculated that it would cost 6 months of one manager's time to prepare all the documentation and procedures necessary for the accreditation. Once you have obtained ISO 9000 you calculate that one manager will have to spend approximately 25 per cent of his or her time maintaining the quality systems and procedures.*

*This meeting has been called to decide whether to try for accreditation.*

**AGENDA**

1. ISO 9000: procedures and systems
2. Advantages and disadvantages
3. Decision and action

*Notes to the agenda*

1. *ISO 9000: procedures and systems*
   The Administration Co-ordinator will briefly present the qualification.
2. *Advantages and disadvantages*
   The meeting will discuss the pros and cons.
3. *Decision and action*
   By the end of the meeting a decision must be taken and any action allocated and scheduled.

# Case Study 18

*Continued...*

## ROLES

### Administration Co-ordinator

If you decide to apply, you need to to hire a consultant for about a week. The consultant will observe the company at work and then make recommendations for changes and, above all, for documentation. One manager will then make sure changes are made. All systems (purchasing, sales, consulting, accounting, etc.) must be documented with lists of procedures, check-lists etc. When the company is ready, a team of assessors will return to assess the quality systems and give approval or not. If not, systems will have to revised and management must then try again. Once accredited, all systems and procedures must be kept up to date. You feel the whole process is too much work.

### Marketing Manager

You are very much in favour of getting ISO 9000. You think it will help to win business and will be very good for the image of the company. It will provide an opportunity for press releases and other public relations activities. You yourself are not a systems man/woman.

### Information Technology Support Manager

You are in favour of getting ISO 9000. You think the systems will help to improve the quality of the service you offer. You think it will help to monitor quality control inside the company. You realize it will be a lot of work but you think it will be worth it.

### Customer Support Manager

You are not in favour of ISO 9000. Your department is already overworked and you don't think it will improve anything to have more documentation and procedures. You don't think it will make much difference in winning contracts. All your customers are much more concerned about the experience of the supplier and the prices they charge.

### Purchasing Manager

You used to work for another company which had ISO 9000 and it was a nightmare. There were hundreds of forms to be filled in and you were surrounded by check-lists. You think the time would be much better spent improving your systems without trying for the accreditation.

### Sales Manager

You think ISO 9000 would be very good for the company and all the employees. It would provide a much clearer framework for working and it would also help to improve the company's image with customers.

# CASE STUDY 19

## Relocation

**ISSUE**

Your company's head office is based in the centre of the capital. The board of your company has decided to relocate it in one of the regions. The management committee now has to meet to discuss the implications of this decision. Rumours about the decision to relocate are already spreading throughout the head office staff (current headcount: 250). It is important that the facts are communicated well and that the committee prepares itself to handle the next 3 months before relocation.

*Facts*

*Date of relocation:* 3 months' time

*Place of relocation:* Purpose-built office block on an industrial estate in the north-east of the country.

*Relocation terms:* All moving costs paid, 3 months' temporary accommodation (hotel), support in finding house.

**AGENDA**

1 **Communication**

2 **Finance**

3 **Support**

4 **Action plan**

*Notes to the agenda*

1 *Communication*
The objective is to decide by whom, how and when the decision to relocate will be communicated to the staff.

2 *Finance*
The objective is to clarify the financial terms for relocation and discuss any possible problems in this area.

3 *Support*
The objective is to identify what sort of support staff will need and to make sure it will be available.

4 *Action plan*
The objective is to allocate responsibility and deadlines for managing the relocation process.

# Case Study 19

## Continued . . .

## ROLES

### Managing Director (Chair)

Your job is to control the meeting and to represent the board. The decision to relocate cannot be changed. You must deal with any discussion about changing the decision firmly. Your objective is to ensure that the company moves to its new location smoothly. You anticipate that approximately 60 per cent of the staff will move. This will mean a radical reorganization but you feel the head office can manage with this sort of cut in staff numbers.

### Public Relations Manager

Your job is to communicate the company's decisions both internally and externally. You know that this decision will be unpopular with a lot of staff. Your job is to persuade them of the advantages (e.g. lower cost of living, better lifestyle, easier transport, etc.). You imagine that not all the staff will be prepared to move but your task is to persuade as many as possible.

### Human Resources Manager

You need to make sure that staff who move are motivated and able to do their jobs. You are aware that the board expects only about 60 per cent of the existing staff to move and sees the relocation partly as a means of reducing staff numbers. You feel it will be very difficult to manage the head office work with such a reduction. You would like to aim for 80 per cent relocation.

### Finance Manager

Your job is keep to the budget for relocation costs. You have calculated the following guidelines.

| Cost per staff member | £ |
|---|---|
| Removal costs | 1,500 |
| Temporary accommodation | 3,000 |
| Travel expenses | 500 |
| Additional support services | 500 |

You are not prepared to see the cost rising above £6,000 per staff member. The total budget is based on 80 per cent of the staff (200) moving.

### Legal Advisor

You work in the legal department. You are concerned that the company treats the workforce fairly and legally. You do not want to move. You feel the company should offer support to those who are not willing to move as well as those who are.

### Administration Manager

You are in charge of many of the head office functions. You are worried that not enough staff will be prepared to move and that the head office will not operate efficiently both before and after the move.

# CASE STUDY 20

## Reorganization

**ISSUE**

*Your company has started a process of 'delayering', or in other words reducing the number of hierarchical levels in the company. The process has implications in a number of areas. First, some jobs have disappeared and this will naturally result in redundancies. Second, many remaining managers will have to accept a slight salary reduction in order to reduce the number of salary grades. Some managers will receive slight increases. Third, there will be no single offices, all of them will have to be shared by at least one other person. This meeting has been called so that the management committee can ensure that the management staff are treated fairly during this painful process.*

**AGENDA**

1. **Job redundancies**
2. **Salary changes**
3. **Office use**
4. **Action plan**

*Notes to the agenda*

1. *Job redundancies*
   The Personnel Manager will briefly present the redundancy plan. The meeting will discuss two or three special cases.
2. *Salary changes*
   The Personnel Manager will explain the main salary changes.
3. *Office use*
   The Administration Manager will briefly present changes to office use.
4. *Action plan*
   Following discussion of the above points, the meeting will decide on the next steps to be taken.

# Case Study 20

## Continued . . .

### ROLES

*Personnel Manager (Chair)*

You have called this meeting to discuss three important issues: redundancies, salary changes and office use.

There will be two compulsory redundancies. Peter Knox is 52 and was offered early retirement. He says he cannot afford to stop working because he has children at college. He would have got a better deal if he had accepted early retirement. The other person is Susan Philips, aged 44. She was offered a transfer but did not accept and is now being made redundant compulsorily. Salary grades are being reduced from five to two. This means that nearly 20 managers will have their salaries reduced by about 2 per cent. Eleven managers will get a salary increase of about 3 per cent. The final objective is to get rid of all closed offices and have one open-plan space. In the interim, ten managers who have previously had their own office will now have to share.

*Finance Manager*

Susan Philips works in your department. Her departure has created a lot of bad feeling. You feel it has been badly managed. Your salary will be cut by 2 per cent, although you will have fewer staff in your department and will therefore have to work harder. You think this is a mistake! You have had your own office for eight years, and you know you will find it very difficult to share with another member of staff.

*Sales Manager*

You have a lot of sympathy for Peter Knox. You have children going through college and you know how expensive it is. You feel the company should have found something for him to do in the new organization. Your salary will be cut by 2 per cent, although you will have fewer staff in your department and will therefore have to work harder. You think this is a mistake! You have had your own office for five years but you understand why it is necessary to share.

*Maintenance Manager*

You have been made redundant twice in your career and you think it's just got to be accepted. Your salary will be increased by 3 per cent, so you are quite happy! You have never had your own office and don't see why anybody should have.

*Production Manager*

You feel sorry for Susan and Peter but, in your opinion, redundancies are part of life.
Your salary will be increased by 3 per cent, so you are quite happy but you can see that salary cuts for some of your colleagues will be demotivating. You have always shared an office and don't spend much time in the office anyway.

# CASE STUDY 21

## The safety committee

**ISSUE**

*Your company has invested a lot of money in safety over the last ten years. Most of the recommendations of the safety committee have been implemented. Recently there has been a change in senior management and a new impetus towards cost-cutting. As a result, the safety committee has been sidelined. On today's agenda you have two important issues of safety and also a chance to discuss the position of the safety committee.*

**AGENDA**

1. Car park lighting
2. Rest room facilities
3. Role of the safety committee
4. Recommendations

*Notes to the agenda*

1. *Car park lighting*

   The staff car park is badly lit. In the winter, this means that drivers can have difficulty seeing people walking to or leaving their cars. It also makes the car park a potentially dangerous place, especially for female members of staff. There have been no incidents in the car park up to now. The cost of installing lights in the car park would be £24,000.

2. *Rest room facilities*

   The company has two rest rooms, one for office staff, the other for production workers. Many of the staff have complained that the facilities are very poor. There is very little space, no comfortable chairs and no natural light from outside. Some members of the safety committee feel a larger room should be used and well furnished and decorated. There is an old workshop in the company grounds. This could be converted to a sort of social club and rest area. Estimated cost of conversion: £85,000.

3. *Role of the safety committee*

   Many of the recommendations of the safety committee are not being acted on. The senior management argue that it is necessary to keep costs tightly under control. Therefore only essential safety obligations will be followed.

4. *Recommendations*

   Following the discussion of the above points, the safety committee will draw up some recommendations to send to senior management.

# Case Study 21

## Continued . . .

### ROLES

*Production Manager*

You are also on the Board of Management and you understand the need for cost-cutting. You feel only essential safety measures should be acted upon. Lighting for the car park is not essential, in your view. It would be nice to have comfortable rest rooms but you don't think it is necessary. On the role of the safety committee, it is important to discuss safety issues and make recommendations. The committee must accept that decisions lie with the board of management.

*Administration Assistant*

You represent the interests of office staff on the safety committee. For many years, staff have complained about the lack of lighting in the car park. You think this investment is essential for the safety and security of all staff. You can see that converting the old workshop to a rest room is probably too expensive. The existing rooms could be improved by better furnishing and decoration. You are willing to look into the cost. The safety committee is vital and you think it should have more power. You would like someone from the legal department on the committee to advise on the legal requirements.

*Maintenance Supervisor*

You represent the interests of the production workers. The car park lighting should be improved but there is no hurry. The rest room for production workers is a disgrace. Very few workers use it and it should be improved as soon as possible. Perhaps the conversion of the workshop could be done in stages, so that the costs could be spread over a number of years. The safety committee does not have enough power, so you would like the senior management to pay more attention to it.

*Production Foreman*

You have just joined the safety committee and your impression is that senior management does not take it seriously. You nearly had an accident last week in the car park when you didn't see someone walking across it. Lighting is essential. The rest rooms need to be improved and you think the conversion of the workshop is a good idea.

*Area Sales Manager*

You have been on the committee for a couple of years and have noticed a change in its power. You know that the market is getting much harder and margins are being squeezed. You have sympathy with the board who are trying to cut costs. You don't think either the car park lighting or the rest room improvement is essential. You are happy with the current role of the safety committee.

*Plant Safety Officer*

You are very unhappy about the declining power of the safety committee. You feel the car park lighting must be improved and, in order to get this acted on, have asked a government safety advisor to come and measure the current lighting levels. The rest rooms need to be renovated urgently. You feel staff cannot be expected to take their breaks in such poor conditions.

# CASE STUDY 22

## Teleworking

**ISSUE**

*Following the breakup of the conglomerate, MegaCorp, many of its business areas have been turned into independent business units. Many of the non-core functions have been outsourced, creating leaner, more profitable and responsive organizations. Technology has dramatically altered many aspects of the organization. Electronic mail gives rapid and cheap communication between the business units and their partners around the globe, and video conterencing is widely used for business meetings. These developments have had a marked influence on the way in which the business units operate. In an effort to maximize the use of manpower and technology, a number of business units are now investigating the use of telecommuting or teleworking, using computers connected by telephone to send and receive work that they do at home.*

**AGENDA**

1. Teleworking activities and company benefits
2. The technical aspects of home working
3. Social effects of home working
4. Supervision of home workers
5. Financial implications

*Notes to the agenda*

1. The consultant will outline the benefits of teleworking.
2. The Operations Director will outline the range of activities which can be carried out from home.
3. The Information Technology Director will present the technical aspects.
4. The Human Resources Director will present the social implications of home working.
5. A Supervisors' Representative will outline plans for supervising home-working.
6. The Finance Director will present the savings.
7. The meeting will decide on a future company policy for teleworking.

# Case Study 22

*Continued . . .*

## ROLES

### Consultant

Teleworking offers excellent opportunities for: more flexible working for the company and its employees; saving on overheads because less desk space required for employees; less time spent on travelling; and greater comfort for employees working from home.

### Operations Director

You believe that the following activities can be carried out at home: data input; data access; and data processing.

In this way, the following operations can be carried out: order processing; generating sales and purchase reports; invoicing; generating reports for management; and purchasing.

As the staff (at present 30 in different departments) concerned with these activities are largely autonomous in their work, they can work equally well at home.

### Information Technology Director

Teleworking sounds very appealing, but you are aware of all the technical problems that you and your team are asked to solve. It would be a mistake to rush into this as there are many problems. Will you solve problems over the phone or will you have to visit the employee's home? How will the installation of new hardware (at present about once per 18 months) be managed? Who will be responsible for training people in the new software?

### Human Resources Director

Over the years, you have seen the gradual isolation of individuals and departments. Many clerical jobs can now be completed alone and many employees spend less time in direct interpersonal communication. This is is one of the reasons for the rapid turnover in staff in certain jobs. Managers, too, are spending less time interacting with each other, as much information can now be called up on their computer screens . All this makes a less healthy working environment. Teleworking seems to be yet another move away from the concept of the organization as a group of people working together.

### Supervisors' Representative

At present the supervisors work very closely with their teams and have built up team spirit. You cannot imagine how you will maintain contact with the individuals in your teams if they are working from home. You feel strongly that teleworking will increase the turnover in administrative jobs and make your job more difficult.

### Finance Director

Under pressure to cut costs, you can see that teleworking offers the possibility to make savings in a number of areas (office space, office furniture, company canteen, etc.) and to allow expansion without investment in additional premises.

# CASE STUDY 23
## Training weekend

**ISSUE**

*Your company recently organized an outdoor weekend to develop teamwork amongst a group of managers. The staff had to do mountain-walking, rock-climbing, canoeing and finally build a bridge over a river. During this last activity one of the team, Doug Walters, suddenly announced that he was not prepared to carry on 'playing these silly games' and left the training centre and drove home. The rest of the group reported that he had seemed tense over the weekend and had clearly not enjoyed the activities. He is an introverted and thoughtful man, very good at his job and well-respected in the company. The weekend had been arranged by the Training Manager who is very much in favour of this type of team-building course. This meeting has been called to discuss Doug and this type of training.*

**AGENDA**

1. Report from Training Manager on weekend and feedback
2. Doug Walters
3. Types and objectives of training
4. Future training policy

*Notes to the agenda*

1. *Report from Training Manager on weekend and feedback*
   The Training Manager will briefly describe the course, objectives and feedback from the other participants.
2. *Doug Walters*
   The Human Resources Manager will update the meeting on Doug Walter's views and feedback from the weekend.
3. *Types and objectives of training*
   A discussion of training policy and plans
4. *Future training policy*
   Any decisions to be taken concerning a change in policy.

# Case Study 23

## Continued . . .

## ROLES

### Human Resources Manager (Chairman)

You have had a meeting with Doug Walters. He said he hates outdoor activities and found the idea of using them for team-building childish and insulting. He is in favour of training but only with concrete objectives. He felt the weekend was a waste of his time and the company's training budget. He apologized for losing his temper and leaving suddenly. He thinks the Training Manager needs to review the objectives of such training.

You are sympathetic to Doug's views although you are in favour of team-building courses. Doug is an excellent employee who contributes a lot on the technical side. People like him should not be forced to participate in such training.

### Training Manager

You carried out a review of the weekend with all the participants except Doug. They enjoyed the weekend and thought it was valuable in building team spirit. You feel this type of outdoor weekend is excellent for motivation and understanding each other. You think Doug is not a team player and is unsuited to the company. Your position is simple. 'If you're not one of the team, then you shouldn't be in the company.'

### R&D Manager

You are Doug Walters' boss. He is one of the most important members of your team. He likes to work on his own but he is always supportive and sympathetic to other members of the team. You don't like the type of training the Training Manager is organizing.

### Sales Manager

You support the Training Manager. You think this type of outdoor training is excellent. You want to send all your sales people on a course. You don't know Doug Walters but, to you, he sounds like 'trouble'.

### Production Manager

Doug has helped the production department a lot in developing new methods. You find him quite difficult to talk to but you value his ideas. You don't have a strong opinion about the training but you feel the company should be able to employ all types of personality.

### Administration Manager

You have had to deal with Doug on a number of occasions. He has often complained about administrative procedures. You found him a difficult person. You feel he needs to adapt more to working with people in an organization.

# CASE STUDY 24

## Workload

**ISSUE**

*Following a reorganization in your company, many staff have complained of the increased workload. The typical working day for managers has become 8 a.m. to 8 p.m. The level of stress amongst many staff has increased and days off due to illness have also increased. Although the company is more competitive (profits are up), the cost in human terms seems very high. Opinions vary amongst senior managers. Some argue that the modern business world is the same for everybody and staff have to learn to take the pressure, others feel that something must be done to reduce workloads.*

*This meeting has been called to discuss the issue and decide if any action needs to be taken.*

**AGENDA**

1. Review of workloads from departmental heads: sales, finance, production and administration
2. Work organization
3. Action

*Notes to the agenda*

1. *Review of workloads from departmental heads: sales, finance, production and administration*

   Each department head should present their view of workloads since the reorganization.

2. *Work organization*

   The Training Manager will talk about some initiatives which could be taken to reduce workloads.

3. *Action*

   The meeting will decide if any action needs to be taken.

# Case Study 24

*Continued . . .*

## ROLES

### General Manager (Chair)

The reorganization was initiated by head office and you are not surprised by the problems it has created. You feel that many of your staff are at breaking point. You have arranged this meeting so that you can hear from all the department heads. Your Training Manager has come prepared to make some suggestions.

### Training Manager

You feel the situation could be improved by various training initiatives:

- time management courses which would help managers to prioritize better
- stress management courses to help managers to be more at ease at work
- strategy and organization courses for senior managers, to improve goal-setting, work allocation and performance assessment.

### Finance Manager

Your department has been cut from 25 to just 15 staff. Some of the accounting work has been taken over by head office but the departmental workload has not decreased that much. You hope that the introduction of new accounting software will help. In the meantime management accounts will certainly be delayed, and there may be problems with cash flow resulting from slower invoicing than usual.

### Sales Manager

Your sales force has not been reduced but the administrative support has been cut from four to two people. Last week one of these two sales assistants was off sick, certainly due to overwork. As a result monthly sales reports are being delayed, and the company can expect this problem to get worse over the coming months.

### Production Manager

Your staff have been reduced by 25 per cent. This is mainly in the area of maintenance, where the work has been outsourced. The maintenance team also used to support the production team when they were short staffed. As a result of the reductions, lead times on order processing have increased by one or two days.

### Administration Manager

Your staff have been decreased from 10 to just 4. Your department is responsible for all the administration support systems, desktop computers, photocopying, post, printing and typing. You used to employ four typists. You now have none and managers have to do all their own typing. The remaining four staff are working extremely hard and you feel that it is only a question of time before they start to take time off for illness.

# STAFF COMMITTEE MEETING 1

*You are a member of a staff committee which meets regularly. Your task is to consider the items and then to make recommendations to the board of directors.*

**AGENDA**

1. Parking
2. Bad weather
3. Smoking
4. Office planning
5. Racial abuse on the shop-floor
6. Early retirement scheme

*Procedure*

After you have read through the 'Notes to the agenda', prepare for the meeting (*see* p. 1):

1. Choose a chairperson for each item. This person will be responsible for introducing the item and chairing the discussion.
2. Decide on the timing for the meeting.
3. Decide on the output of the meeting (minutes, action plan, etc.).

# Staff Committee Meeting 1

*Continued . . .*

---

**NOTES TO THE AGENDA**

## 1 Parking

The company car park is not large enough. The management have a section of the car park reserved for them. This is often half full as a lot of managers are away from the office. Employees who can't find a place have to park quite a long way from the company and sometimes have to pay for parking. Some staff have suggested the whole car park should be available to all employees on a 'first come, first served' basis. Some managers argue that their jobs are less 9 to 5 and they need to have a place reserved for them.

## 2 Bad weather

This winter there has been some very severe weather. Sometimes it has been difficult and dangerous to get to work. Some staff have suggested that the company should allow employees to stay at home on such days, with no loss of pay. Does such as system need to be formalized or should the unwritten rule be 'If you can possibly get to work, do so!'?

## 3 Smoking

The company banned smoking from all offices one year ago. Smokers now go out of the building to smoke. These smokers go to the front entrance. They often need several minutes to get there and then the same to return to their offices. Should smoking be banned around the building as well? Providing smoking areas in the company will be expensive and go against the policy introduced one year ago.

## 4 Office planning

A few years ago the company moved from closed offices to an open-plan workspace. Most staff have adapted to this change but some (about 15 per cent) have found it very difficult to work in this environment. They complain that they cannot concentrate and their work has suffered. One solution would be to section off one part of the workspace as a 'quiet area'. Alternatively, some closed offices could be reconstructed.

## 5 Racial abuse on the shop-floor

The factory workforce is composed of black and white workers. Recently there have been complaints from a few black workers of racial abuse from one of the factory foremen. The Production Manager has investigated the complaints. The workers say they have been called names. The foreman denies it. The Production Manager reckons that the foreman is racist and would not be surprised if he had racially abused the other workers.

## 6 Early retirement scheme

The company introduced an early retirement scheme for people over 55 last year. Many workers have now left the company using this scheme. Ironically, many new temporary workers have been employed often in their late fifties or early sixties. The staff feel the company has used the scheme to change the workforce from permanent full-time staff to temporary, part-time staff. Business has picked up since the scheme was introduced and there has been a need to recruit more staff. Management argues that they had to lose staff one year ago and the early retirement scheme was the best way of doing so.

# STAFF COMMITTEE MEETING 2

*You are a member of a staff committee which meets regularly. Your task is to consider the items and then to make recommendations to the board of directors.*

**AGENDA**

1. Illness
2. Age barrier
3. Client lunches
4. Secretarial work
5. Charity sponsorship
6. Community work

*Procedure*

After you have read through the 'Notes to the agenda', prepare for the meeting (*see* p. 1):

1. Choose a chairperson for each item. This person will be responsible for introducing the item and chairing the discussion.
2. Decide on the timing for the meeting.
3. Decide on the output of the meeting (minutes, action plan, etc.).

# Staff Committee Meeting 2

*Continued . . .*

---

**NOTES TO THE AGENDA**

### 1 Illness

Levels of absenteeism have increased in the company. This has been mainly caused by an increase in sick leave. In winter many more people have been taking time off work because of illness. Some people believe absenteeism is increasing because of stress at work, others because employees are less loyal to the company. The committee needs to come up with some suggestions for solving this problem.

### 2 Age barrier

New managerial jobs and promotions in general are being given to young employees or recruits in their 30s. There are fewer opportunities for men and women in their late 40s and 50s. The age structure of the company is gradually being changed. Is this a problem? Don't we need to encourage and motivate older employees?

### 3 Client lunches

Visiting customers and other contacts used to be taken to the company's canteen for lunch. Now they are taken to an expensive restaurant in town. Their hosts say that the food in the canteen is not good enough and that the atmosphere is better in the restaurant for talking business. What does the committee think about this development?

### 4 Secretarial work

The number of secretaries has been cut in the company. Part of the justification was that managers should do more of their own word-processing on their computers. Some managers continue to request reports and other documents to be typed by overworked secretaries. The secretaries complain that is difficult to say 'no', because the managers are more senior.

### 5 Charity sponsorship

The company has given a lot of money to a local charity which works with homeless young people. The Marketing Manager, who originally proposed this charity, is married to the woman who runs the local homeless shelter. The company's charity contributions mean the shelter can employ this woman full-time. Some people feel that other charities should be supported, but, if the support to the homeless charity is reduced, the shelter might have to close.

### 6 Community work

Employees of the company are encouraged to get involved in community projects and the company allows them time off work to help in the community. A recent project has involved renovating some old farm buildings to provide a social centre for local inhabitants. The local council has now asked for a drainage pipe to be removed from the land. This pipe drains waste water from the company's production process and moving it would cost £50,000. If the council forces the company to move the pipe, the board might consider stopping this sort of community work.

# STAFF COMMITTEE MEETING 3

*You are a member of a staff committee which meets regularly. Your task is to consider the items and then to make recommendations to the board of directors.*

**AGENDA**

1. Social club: equal opportunities
2. Christmas party
3. Company car policy
4. Internet use
5. Perk or corruption
6. Performance appraisal

*Procedure*

After you have read through the 'Notes to the agenda', prepare for the meeting (*see* p. 1):

1. Choose a chairperson for each item. This person will be responsible for introducing the item and chairing the discussion.
2. Decide on the timing for the meeting.
3. Decide on the output of the meeting (minutes, action plan, etc.).

# Staff Committee Meeting 3

*Continued . . .*

---

**NOTES TO THE AGENDA**

### 1 Social club: equal opportunities

Many female employees are not at ease in the company social club. It is dominated by men; they play pool, drink, smoke and have a good time. Women sit in a dark corner away from everybody else. There are now more female employees than male employees in the company. Men who use the social club are very happy with it. Should it be changed? If so, how?

### 2 Christmas party

The company always holds a Christmas party for the children of all the employees. It is very expensive, with presents, entertainment and a big lunch for the children and the parents. It has been suggested that the money spent on the party could be given to a local orphanage where the children have very little. The company cannot afford to do both.

### 3 Company car policy

Your company has always bought domestically produced company cars. This year the purchasing department is considering buying cars from other countries. They have been offered a good deal and want to get the best deal for the company, without letting national sentiment get in the way.

### 4 Internet use

All employees with desktop computers now have access to the Internet. It was expected that the company's phone bills would drop as fax was used less and e-mail more. In fact, telephone bills have increased by 30 per cent as employees spend long periods searching on the Internet. Should the Internet access be stopped? Who should have access to the Internet?

### 5 Perk or corruption

One of the perks (benefits) of some jobs are the gifts received from suppliers. At Christmas, the purchasing department receive all sorts of gifts ranging from pens to bottles of wine. Occasionally, they receive gifts such as short breaks in hotels, free dinners and entertainment. Should the purchasing department share these gifts around the company or keep them to themselves? Should the gifts go to better causes, for example a local charity? Should suppliers be discouraged from sending gifts?

### 6 Performance appraisal

For two years the company has operated a system of performance appraisal. Each employee is appraised by his or her boss, and training, promotion opportunity and salary rises are agreed. It has been suggested that the company should also operate 'upward appraisal' where the bosses are appraised by their subordinates. Does the committee think this is a good idea? If so, how would it be implemented?

# STAFF COMMITTEE MEETING 4

*You are a member of a staff committee which meets regularly. Your task is to consider the items and then to make recommendations to the board of directors.*

**AGENDA**

1 **Nuclear industry administration**
2 **Employment dilemma**
3 **Racial harassment**
4 **Sponsorship**
5 **Pilfering**
6 **A question of drink**

*Procedure*

After you have read through the 'Notes to the agenda', prepare for the meeting (*see* p. 1):

1. Choose a chairperson for each item. This person will be responsible for introducing the item and chairing the discussion.
2. Decide on the timing for the meeting.
3. Decide on the output of the meeting (minutes, action plan, etc.).

# Staff Committee Meeting 4

## Continued . . .

**NOTES TO THE AGENDA**

*1 Nuclear industry administration*

Your company has always had an image of environmental friendliness. A major nuclear reprocessing company is coming to your town. Many of the small local companies are launching a campaign to prevent them from setting up. The relocation would bring new jobs and increase your business. You seek the committee's views on whether you should join the campaign against the relocation.

*2 Employment dilemma*

A government scheme is offering financial subsidies to encourage companies to employ recently-released convicts. Your company would pay 50 per cent of the wage and the government would match this. You would like the committee's views on the principle of employing ex-convicts, the practical aspects of identifying suitable job areas, the effect on other employees, and steps to integrate them smoothly into the company.

*3 Racial harassment*

Some of the production workers belong to ethnic minorities. They are hard workers, keep themselves to themselves, and in some cases, hardly speak any of the local language (English). Yesterday, one of them complained because she was asked to do boring jobs. In addition, she said that there had been verbal abuse from other workers.

*4 Sponsorship*

Your company has always had a good relationship with the local community. You contribute to a number of charitable organizations and local cultural events. You have been approached by the festival committee to contribute towards the annual fair. This usually takes the form of singing, dancing and other cultural events. It is a local holiday and most of the residents come to watch the celebrations. The advance programme shows an event to commemorate Theodore Poster. He was a charismatic local figure who kept the local population ethnically pure. Nothing was ever proved against him, but you are very concerned. You would like the committee's views on whether you should continue to support the festival.

*5 Pilfering*

Over the years many items of minor value have gone missing from the company's premises, often no more than stationery. Now there is the regular disappearance of photocopy paper, pens, pencils and other items. Last week one of the staff told you that her handbag had been stolen. The police were informed, wrote down the details, but took no further action.

*6 A question of drink*

Albert Brown has been with the company for 25 years. He has worked his way up from an office cleaner to a supervisor on the shop-floor responsible for 25 workers. Two weeks ago, you called Albert into your office for a meeting, and you clearly smelt alcohol on his breath. At that time you didn't say anything. Yesterday, you heard that he had come to work drunk and had hit another worker. You have heard from another shop-floor worker that Albert's wife left him some months ago.

# STAFF COMMITTEE MEETING 5

*You are a member of a staff committee which meets regularly. Your task is to consider the items and then to make recommendations to the Board of Directors.*

**AGENDA**

1. A question of lateness
2. Sexual harassment
3. Keeping fit
4. Job titles
5. Time-keeping
6. The photocopier

*Procedure*

After you have read through the 'Notes to the agenda', prepare for the meeting (*see* p. 1):

1. Choose a chairperson for each item. This person will be responsible for introducing the item and chairing the discussion.
2. Decide on the timing for the meeting.
3. Decide on the output of the meeting (minutes, action plan, etc.).

# Staff Committee Meeting 5

*Continued . . .*

---

**NOTES TO THE AGENDA**

### 1  A question of lateness

Susan Marham is an excellent personal assistant. She is very competent in the office and manages her own workload, as well as yours, very efficiently. However, she is always late in the mornings, when you need someone to answer the phone as there are regular calls from abroad. You have talked to her many times about this and she always promises to be at the office on time, but doesn't do so. Last week you lost a major contract because a client couldn't get through to you or your secretary. You know that Susan is a single mother and has two young children aged 3 and 5.

### 2  Sexual harassment

Maggie Brown takes great care over her appearance and clearly spends a lot of money on expensive clothes. In a group she enjoys getting the attention of her male colleagues, especially the Managing Director. Yesterday, she complained to you that the boss had sexually harassed her by suggesting that they spend the night together. You were very surprised because you thought that Maggie could handle a little joke, but she was clearly upset.

### 3  Keeping fit

Last year one of your competitors introduced a morning keep fit class for all company employees. Although there was a lot of scepticism at first, the session, offered to all workers for 30 minutes before the morning shift, is now very popular. Unfortunately, there have been a number of minor casualties from over-enthusiastic participants. You are wondering whether to introduce a similar programme and would like the committee's views about the advantages and disadvantages.

### 4  Job titles

Your company has always been proud of its flat company organization and policy of open communication. However, as it has gone international, many of the new foreign clients have been surprised that staff do not have clear job titles. As a result, some senior managerial titles have been created in order to avoid confusion among clients. You have now heard that some of the subordinate staff would like to have clear job titles, too.

### 5  Time-keeping

Your office has always been fairly free and easy about time. As long as the work gets done, you trusted people to manage their own time. Now you've noticed that people are beginning to arrive late and go home early, not only in your office, but in other offices, too. You would like the committee's views on the importance of timekeeping and what steps, if any, should be taken.

### 6  The photocopier

The photocopier is an essential resource in your office and you get valuable service from it. However, you are always horrified to see how many copies are wasted and how much paper is thrown away. Is there really unnecessary usage and what steps, if any, can be taken to use it less wastefully?

# STAFF COMMITTEE MEETING 6

*You are a member of a staff committee which meets regularly. Your task is to consider the items and then to make recommendations to the Board of Directors.*

**AGENDA**

1. Reference for incompetent employee
2. A new personal assistant
3. Libel
4. Firing
5. The argumentative couple
6. Office temperature

*Procedure*

After you have read through the 'Notes to the agenda', prepare for the meeting (*see* p. 1):

1. Choose a chairperson for each item. This person will be responsible for introducing the item and chairing the discussion.
2. Decide on the timing for the meeting.
3. Decide on the output of the meeting (minutes, action plan, etc.).

# Staff Committee Meeting 6

*Continued . . .*

---

**NOTES TO THE AGENDA**

*1 Reference for incompetent employee*

You were very relieved when Roger Dixon finally left the company some 3 months ago. His work as quality supervisor had been poor and he had made some expensive mistakes. As you had been his boss, you had agreed to act as referee for him. You have now been asked to write a reference on Roger, who has applied to be quality manager for one of your suppliers.

*2 A new personal assistant*

You recently advertised in the local press for a personal assistant. The best application for the post was from a candidate in her late twenties. She came for an interview and impressed you with her administrative and secretarial skills. You are concerned that, as she's engaged to be married, she may want to leave and start a family before long. You therefore wonder whether you should appoint your second choice.

*3 Libel*

At a recent Chamber of Commerce lunch, one of your subordinates, who had had too much to drink, started making offensive and insensitive remarks about the company and its senior management. Naturally, some of the listeners were amused; others were disgusted by his behaviour. You wonder what action should be taken, if any, and by whom.

*4 Firing*

You have recently been appointed as a junior manager and are keen to do the job well. Two of the staff that you have inherited have failed to meet your expectations and you have no other alternative but to fire them.

*5 The argumentative couple*

Two members of your staff, both of who are in line for promotion, are constantly having rows and scoring points off each other. It has become an office joke, but you don't think it's good for their work nor for the office atmosphere.

*6 Office temperature*

The statutory minimum temperature for offices is 20°C. However, when some of the office staff complained they were cold, you increased it to 22°C. Now you are getting complaints that the offices are too hot. As you are housed in a modern office block, the office temperature is regulated centrally and the windows can't be opened.

# STAFF COMMITTEE MEETING 7

*You are a member of a staff committee which meets regularly. Your task is to consider the items and then to make recommendations to the Board of Directors.*

**AGENDA**

1. **Rumours**
2. **Non-contributory manager**
3. **Woman's role**
4. **Entertaining clients**
5. **Office parties**
6. **Freelancing**

*Procedure*

After you have read through the 'Notes to the agenda', prepare for the meeting (*see* p. 1):

1. Choose a chairperson for each item. This person will be responsible for introducing the item and chairing the discussion.
2. Decide on the timing for the meeting.
3. Decide on the output of the meeting (minutes, action plan, etc.).

# Staff Committee Meeting 7

*Continued...*

---

**NOTES TO THE AGENDA**

*1 Rumours*

You have heard one of your subordinates discussing confidential board-level information with other junior managers. The discussion centred around speculation about the company's future, especially a takeover by a competitor. You would like the committee's views on whether you should take action to try to prevent harmful rumours being spread. And if so, what action would be appropriate?

*2 Non-contributory manager*

You work as marketing manager, responsible for a team of regional sales managers. In your regular weekly sales meetings with the regional managers, there is one manager who never says anything. His sales results are good and you have no concern about his performance. However, you are worried that he doesn't contribute to the meetings.

*3 Woman's role*

You are the only woman in a group of middle managers, and at the regular meetings it is expected that you will take notes or minutes. Recently, you have been asked to make a cup of tea or coffee for the meeting participants. You feel that it is wrong for the other middle managers to automatically expect you to do these tasks just because you are a woman.

*4 Entertaining clients*

As marketing manager, you have to entertain clients several times a week. You often take them out for lunch to a rather expensive restaurant. You usually take a three-course meal with wine, which gives both of you an opportunity to discuss areas of business without rushing. You generally end the meeting feeling satisfied with the results. On the other hand, work is impossible afterwards and this makes you feel bad. You would like the committee's guidelines on how to achieve the same business results, but without the overindulgence.

*5 Office parties*

As office manager, you have noted the increasing time and money spent on office parties. These celebrate company successes, national holidays, and employees' birthdays. They are clearly good for the morale of the company and are often cited jokingly by employees as a reason for the company's success. You would like the committee's guidelines on what events should be celebrated.

*6 Freelancing*

You are responsible for personnel at a management training consultancy. For the training courses you offer, you often use the services of outside consultants. As these consultants also work for your competitors, you are worried that they will pass on sensitive information about your organization and about your clients.

# STAFF COMMITTEE MEETING 8

You are a member of a staff committee which meets regularly. Your task is to consider the items and then to make recommendations to the Board of Directors.

**AGENDA**

1. Financial services
2. Chemical leak
3. Sex and drugs
4. Compensation
5. Anti-ageing cream
6. Workload

*Procedure*

After you have read through the 'Notes to the agenda', prepare for the meeting (*see* p. 1):

1. Choose a chairperson for each item. This person will be responsible for introducing the item and chairing the discussion.
2. Decide on the timing for the meeting.
3. Decide on the output of the meeting (minutes, action plan, etc.).

# Staff Committee Meeting 8

*Continued . . .*

---

**NOTES TO THE AGENDA**

### 1 *Financial services*

You are a small, successful producer of environmentally-friendly products. You have been approached by EthFin, a financial services company, which offers a range of financial services, all supposedly 'ethical'. At present you are looking for a loan in order to expand. EthFin's terms for the loan are less attractive than those offered by your existing bank. However, you feel that using EthFin could help reinforce your image in the market-place.

### 2 *Chemical leak*

Your production department has told you that there was a minor leak of dangerous chemicals into the local river last week. Last year, when a similar mistake happened, the local environmentalists found out. They told the press and, after a high profile court case, your company was fined and told to improve procedures. You agreed to spend a large sum of money on waste treatment. Some of the new equipment has been installed. The present leak, though much smaller than last year, is likely to cause minor damage to wild life.

### 3 *Sex and drugs*

Your flamboyant Managing Director has often been at the centre of controversy. He is very popular with shareholders, and the value of the company's shares has risen dramatically since he took over.

Now there is a rumour that a reporter from the tabloid newspaper *Famous Secrets* found him at a 'Sex and Drugs' party last week. You are worried that this could have devastating effects on the company's image.

### 4 *Compensation*

Recently a keyboard operator won £1m compensation from her employer for the occupational nerve disease of repetitive strain injury (RSI). The case was followed by a government report highlighting the risks and recommending guidelines for maximum daily hours to be spent working on a keyboard. You have now received a letter from the doctor of one of your employees suggesting that she is suffering from RSI. Her supervisor tells you that the number of hours she spends working on the keyboard are within the government guidelines.

### 5 *Anti-ageing cream*

Your company is a leading producer of anti-ageing cream. In a sector which is surrounded by a lot of hype, your products are well respected in the market-place. You launched 'YoungSkin' about 6 months ago. It was an immediate success. The instructions for use warn of the possibility of irritation, but there have been, as always, a small number of consumer complaints. These have now been thoroughly investigated by your R & D department. They have reported that the risk of 'YoungSkin' causing serious irritation is 0.1 per cent.

### 6 *Workload*

One of your best sales managers told you yesterday that he might leave. He cited family and claimed that because of the long hours and frequent absences, his wife and children rarely saw him. He also told you that his job was important for his financial security and for his self-fulfilment. Naturally, you are very reluctant to let him go.

# SPECIALIST AGENDA 1

## Management

**ISSUE**

GIM, or the Global Institute of Management, plays an influential role in the world of business management. With members in over 100 countries, it regularly:

- organizes international conferences
- produces more than 250 publications
- arranges local workshops
- examines candidates for the GIM Diploma (an internationally recognized management qualification).

On the eve of the millennium, one of the main challenges facing GIM is to bring together the main views and experiences of its many members throughout the world. In fact, though advances in technology have brought managers closer together, views on management still seem to be very far apart.

In an effort to find an acceptable definition of management, GIM has invited 'experts' from a number of key local GIM offices to a meeting (the first truly global meeting of the association) to decide on a wording to be used in GIM's logo after the year 2000. The wording should reflect the key concerns of management in the next century.

**AGENDA**

1. **Management: knowledge or skills?**
2. **Can management be taught?**
3. **A definition of management for GIM**

*Notes to the agenda*

1. *Management: knowledge or skills?*
   Is management based on knowledge of principles or on the application of skills?
   Each manager presents their views.
2. *Can management be taught?*
   Can this knowledge or these skills be taught?
   Each manager presents their views.
3. *A definition of management for GIM*
   The participants agree a wording for the GIM logo.

# Specialist Agenda 1

*Continued . . .*

## ROLES

### Manager 1

Your views on management follow Henri Fayol, the founder of the classical management school. You have spent many years in production management and believe that the key to successful management is forecasting, planning, organizing, commanding, co-ordinating and controlling.

### Manager 2

You believe that, above all, a manager needs to have specialist technical knowledge from his or her field. Specialists know their jobs thoroughly and can make decisions accordingly. Your strength, you believe, is the in-depth knowledge that you have gained in financial management from many years of work in the area.

### Manager 3

In today's business world, no manager can carry out all the tasks without the support of an able team. Team-working is the key to success. And for team-working to be effective, any manager needs to be able to delegate tasks. You believe that you have developed the skills to be a good delegator and this has enabled you to work effectively as a manager in a number of industries.

### Manager 4

You believe that management is about attitudes. If you have the right attitude, then you can achieve success. Your views follow Tom Peters' and you believe that effective managers get their organizational direction from 'sound common sense, pride in the organization and enthusiasm for its works'.

### Manager 5

You believe that the best managers have well-balanced personalities. You believe that the optimal mix should include ambition, commitment, energy and physical and psychological stability.

### Manager 6

You believe that the most important skill for managers is to be able to motivate their colleagues. No manager can accomplish everything alone. He or she needs a team. To gain the commitment of the team and achieve the organization's goals, the manager needs to be able to motivate them.

# SPECIALIST AGENDA 2

## Quality

**ISSUE**

It has been a bad year for fairgrounds. They have been under increasing pressure from other leisure industry providers. As a result, fairground operators have been forced to cut costs, especially on the maintenance of the rides. In addition, the 'big dipper' and the 'freefall', two of the most popular rides, have come in for criticism after two high profile accidents earlier this year. No one was seriously injured, but these accidents are always headline news. They also have the effect of giving all funfairs a bad name. As a result of this and the trend towards other leisure pursuits, attendances at funfairs have been slowly dropping off throughout the country.

In an attempt to reverse the falling numbers, a special quality group has been set up. The group consists of the representatives from the main fairground operators. Your task is to create a new quality statement for fairgrounds.

In this first meeting, the aim is to consider the key aspects of quality. These will then be drafted in a document which will be released to the press and the media. The objective of this first stage is to reassure the general public of the intentions of the fairground operators to clean up their act. The second stage, for a subsequent meeting, is to establish a code of conduct for all members of the fairground operators' association. In this way a set of standards will be introduced for the first time into this sector of the leisure industry in order to provide 'objectively measurable safety criteria for all of our customers'.

Your task for the meeting is to agree on a statement which defines a quality standard for fairground operators.

**AGENDA**

1. The problems of the industry
2. The importance of quality
3. The scope of quality
4. A definition of quality for the fairground industry

*Notes to the agenda*

1. *The problems of the industry*
   Each operator outlines their view of the problems.
2. *The importance of quality*
   Each operator presents their view of the importance of quality for the industry.
3. *The scope of quality*
   Each operator explains what aspects quality needs to cover.
4. *A definition of quality for the fairground industry*
   The participants agree a wording for the quality statement.

# Specialist Agenda 2

*Continued . . .*

---

**ROLES**

*Operator 1*

You believe that customers have become more concerned about quality. This includes, particularly, the quality of the staff, the quality of the equipment, the quality of the maintenance and the quality of the safety standards. You think that the quality statement should prominently display the groups concern with these quality issues. You favour a statements such as 'Quality is number 1.'

*Operator 2*

Fairground operators, like yourself, have been under a lot of financial pressure recently. The business has become more competitive. Equipment and personnel have both become more expensive. It is true that some operators have tried to cut corners by saving money, wherever possible. You believe that the quality statement needs to put the customer centre-stage. You favour a statement such as 'Customers are our focus.'

*Operator 3*

You believe that, in the customers' minds, fairground are above all about fun. Like other leisure sector providers, you need to attract clients by giving them what they want. You believe that this is a quality service in a leisure context. You favour a statement such as 'Quality is our most important service.'

*Operator 4*

The increasing costs of equipment and maintenance is making it more difficult to make a profit. One response has been to cut running costs by rationalizing the number of fairground workers. The result has been fewer workers and longer hours. This has created a bad image and, in your mind, led to some accidents. You believe that the industry needs to raise its standards by investing more in people. You believe that this will help to raise the industry's profile. You favour a statement such as 'Quality is employee involvement.'

*Operator 5*

The fairground is becoming more sophisticated, and customers are becoming more demanding. The newer rides make use of the latest technology and computer control systems. The younger customers are no longer satisfied with the traditional 'rides'. You are sure that new equipment will bring the customers back. In any case, the newer equipment is now much safer. If you can show the customer that you are replacing old equipment, they will be reassured about quality standards. You favour a statement such as 'Our mission is to constantly improve our services to meet customer needs.'

*Operator 6*

In your experience quality is not a cost. It doesn't come from investing in expensive equipment or highly-qualified workers. Quality comes from developing the right attitudes. With these right attitudes come improved standards of working. You favour a statement such as 'Quality is free.'

# SPECIALIST AGENDA 3

## Human resources (1)

**ISSUE**

*Management practices develop in response to the changing demands of the organizations that they serve. One key example is human resources, which has grown far beyond its original concerns for the welfare of employees. In the process, it has forsaken its concerns for the workforce, and is today seen as more concerned for the company's bottom line.*

*So, what are the legitimate concerns for the human resources professional? In an attempt to find an answer to this question, a meeting of human resources specialists has been convened to define the scope of human resources. The participants have been chosen because of their wide-ranging and different views on human resources.*

**AGENDA**

1. The demands of today's organization
2. The scope of human resources management
3. A definition of human resources management

*Notes to the agenda*

1. *The demands of today's organizations*
   Each specialist presents their view on what drives today's organizations.
2. *The scope of human resources management*
   Each specialist presents their view of human resources management (see 'Roles').
3. *A definition of human resources management*
   The participants agree a wording for the scope of human resources management.

# Specialist Agenda 3

*Continued . . .*

## ROLES

*Specialist 1*

You believe that the main function of human resources is to support the company's employees. With the current trends towards rationalization and downsizing, many employees are in danger of losing their basic rights.

*Specialist 2*

In your opinion, human resources has a wide function. It exists to formulate the 'values' of the organization: to set out the type of employer that it intends to be and to define the management style.

*Specialist 3*

Organizations exist, above all, to make a profit for their shareholders. Central to this objective is having the right people. You believe that the scope of human resources management is to quantify the manpower needs of the organization in order to maximize and optimize its operations.

*Specialist 4*

Every organization needs people. And both the organization and its people need to 'grow' – the organization in size, and the people in terms of personal and professional development. In your opinion, the role of human resources management is to develop the company's employees, which will then be translated into increased profits, service quality and organizational stability.

*Specialist 5*

In today's business environment, every organization requires teamwork. The most successful companies are those which provide a supportive climate for their people. You believe that the central role for human resources specialists is to support managers throughout the organization so that they can be more effective people managers.

*Specialist 6*

The demands of the workplace are changing more quickly than at any time in history. This means that today's employees regularly need new knowledge and skills. The job of the Human Resources Manager is to ensure that the workforce is competent, up-to-date, motivated and fully developed.

# SPECIALIST AGENDA 4

## Promotion

### ISSUE

Promoting a new product or service can be a very costly exercise, as Slimmers' Health Club are just finding out. After a successful launch 6 months ago, the number of regular users has started to drop off. The three directors are getting worried.

Located in the centre of Newtown's commercial district, the club should be well placed to pick up business from busy executives, in need of a workout – either during their lunch break or after work. In fact, the club has gone to great lengths to provide the right facilities for this market and a flexible membership scheme. The main competition comes from two other well-established health centres, but their customers have complained that the equipment is often over-subscribed and the exercise areas too full. A new club would be well placed to pick up the overcapacity. However, it is clear that more needs to be done to bring in the customers – or perhaps to look for other customers.

Therefore, a team of three advertising consultants have been invited to advise on the different types of promotional strategies that you could adopt within your budget of £3,000.

### AGENDA

1. The problems of Slimmers' Health Club
2. The role of promotion
3. The opportunities provided by promotional tools
4. Action plan for Slimmers' Health Club

*Notes to the agenda*

1. *The problems of Slimmers' Health Club*
   The directors present the problems facing the club.
2. *The role of promotion*
   The consultants present the role and benefits of promotion.
3. *The opportunities provided by promotional tools*
   Each participant presents their favoured approach.
4. *Action plan for Slimmers' Health Club*
   The participants agree on an action plan.

# Specialist Agenda 4

*Continued . . .*

---

## ROLES

### Director 1, Slimmers' Health Club

You believe that the main problem facing the club is that not enough people know of its existence. You feel sure that promotion will help to raise awareness in the community. To achieve that, you favour investing in the sponsorship of a local sports or fitness event at a cost of £1,000.

### Director 2, Slimmers' Health Club

The core of your present business comes from a small number of regular users. They have subscribed as members. In addition, you have a number of casual users who exercise once or twice a month, preferring to pay a high hourly rate rather than joining the club. You believe that you need to increase membership by persuading the casual users to become members. You think the best way to do this is through a special offer of reduced membership rates. You estimate that this would cost you £1,000.

### Director 3, Slimmers' Health Club

The business community is where your customers come from. Therefore, you believe that you must have more contact with them. You favour a special personal selling campaign to local companies which might be interested in corporate membership. The campaign would cost in the region of £1,000.

### Advertising consultant 1

You have helped many small businesses in the local community before, although health clubs are a new area for you. You have tried many promotional tools and you have found direct mailing to potential customers to be the most successful. You could provide a well-targeted mailing for £1,500.

### Advertising consultant 2

You are a keen sports person and a member of one of the competing clubs. You feel that the name 'Slimmers' Health Club' will put a lot of potential customers off. The focus should be on exercise and its benefits, not on the weight problems of the users. You advised a competitor club during its setup and found that point-of-sale advertising at shops which sell sports wear was a very successful promotional tool. You could provide a similar service to Slimmers' Health Club for £1,000.

### Advertising consultant 3

You believe that the key to success lies in reaching a wider audience interested in sports and fitness. These audiences can be reached by advertising at events which attract large numbers of people. You have in mind the local football matches and other sporting activities. Perimeter advertising for a season would cost about £1,000 per location.

# SPECIALIST AGENDA 5

## The training dilemma

**ISSUE**

'We need more training.'

The Training Manager at a large multinational oil company was delighted to hear the Human Resources Director make this pronouncement at a recent meeting. But, he went on to say, the whole training department should be made redundant and then outsourced, because full-time, in-house trainers are inefficient. The Human Resources Director then identified the types of training that he felt were the key to the company's successful future:

- specialist technical skills training for marketing, finance, production, etc.
- generic management training for team-building, leadership and project management
- information technology skills training for handling the new equipment and software
- communication skills training in areas such as presentations, meetings and report-writing.

In order to resolve the issues, a meeting has been called to look at the training function and the options.

**AGENDA**

1. **The purpose of training: presented by the Human Resources Director and outside consultant**
2. **The types of courses currently offered: presented by the Training Manager**
3. **The deliverers of training: presented by the trainers and the Training Manager**
4. **Review of policy and action: all members**

*Notes to the agenda*

1. *The purpose of training*
   The Human Resources Director and the outside consultant present their views of the purpose of training.
2. *The types of courses currently offered*
   The Training Manager presents the types of training currently on offer.
3. *The deliverers of training*
   The trainers and the Training Manager describe the present situation for training delivery.
4. *Review of policy and action*
   All the participants review the present policy and decide whether a change of policy is required.
5. *Action*
   The participants decide on any action required to implement any changes in policy.

# Specialist Agenda 5

*Continued . . .*

## ROLES

### Human Resources Director (Chair)

You made your views clear at the meeting last month. All training should be outsourced. This is the only way to maintain your company's present position as a world-class player. The current training practices are expensive, inefficient and prevent the company from achieving its goals. Your opinions of in-house trainers are:

1. To use them effectively, they need to spend 70 per cent of their time in the classroom; this leads to quick burnout.
2. They are difficult to manage; they are a quirky group of individuals, rather than team players.
3. Most of them are not interested in, or do not understand the business; they quickly become inward-looking and fail to respond to organizational needs.

### Outside Consultant

There is a need for a small group of trainers to be kept within the organization. Many of the generic courses, such as management development, communication skills training and information technology can be outsourced. However, there is valuable knowledge built up by trainers working within areas such as marketing, finance and production. It would be difficult to find this type of trainer outside the company.

### Training Manager

You have worked hard to put the present training team together. You have agreed a wide range of contracts, ranging from full-time to hourly paid, so you don't think that the criticism of expense is justified. Trainers also work on valuable areas such as resource development. You have a good team, able to deliver excellent courses throughout the company. The feedback from course participants usually ranges from good to excellent. Finally, you know that with outsourcing, your job might be cut, as the training management functions could be carried out by an administrative assistant.

### Training Co-ordinator

You reject the Human Resources Director's comment that the in-house trainers are simply a group of individuals. Of course, there are some interesting characters among them, but that is in the nature of training. You have worked on training development, so that you have a reliable, professional, committed training team.

### Trainer (1)

You have been employed by the company for 10 years and have seen your training hours rise from 10 a week to more than 20 a week now. This is an exhausting workload. You appreciate the security of full-time employment, but believe that you could continue to work inside the company on a freelance basis. Your knowledge and skills will be needed in the future; and you would benefit from fewer hours and higher pay.

### Trainer (2)

You have recently joined the in-house team, bringing with you a high degree of energy and enthusiasm. You are worried about the potential outsourcing of the training, as you think it would be difficult to find another job quickly. In any case, you like the team working and the opportunities for professional exchange with other trainers.

# SPECIALIST AGENDA 6

## Sales and marketing

**ISSUE**

*You all work in the marketing department of a large international company which manufactures security systems. Recently your company launched a new product called 'The Max'. It is a sophisticated alarm system which also photographs any intruders. To launch the product you used a TV advertising campaign loosely based on a film called Mad Max. There has been a public outcry, with parts of the media arguing that the film seeks to terrify people into buying alarm systems. The meeting has been called to discuss the campaign.*

**AGENDA**

1. The Max campaign
2. Sales report
3. Public relations report
4. Review of policy and action

*Notes to the agenda*

1. *The Max campaign*
   The Marketing Manager will report on the concepts behind the campaign and its results
2. *Sales report*
   The Sales Manager will report on sales since the launch.
3. *Public relations report*
   The Public Relations Manager will report on press relations and other PR issues.
4. *Review of policy and action*
   The meeting will decide whether any action needs to be taken.

# Specialist Agenda 6

## Continued . . .

**ROLES**

*Marketing Manager (Chair)*

You were responsible for giving the advertising agency the go-ahead to film the 'Mad Max' commercial. Personally you think it is a fantastic ad and rather dramatically sells the features of the Max Alarm system. You also feel that the bad publicity will not harm the company in the end. It certainly will increase sales.

*Sales Manager*

You are delighted with the impact of the ad. Sales of the Max system have doubled in the last two months and the main problem is producing enough to meet demand. You can see that the ad might offend some people but there have been no complaints about the product and that is the important thing.

*Public Relations Manager*

You feel you should have been consulted about the ad. It has been a disaster for the company. Your phone has not stopped ringing with local and national press asking for the company's position. Most of the press have criticized the ad. They say it is designed to frighten people and they feel elderly people in particular might confuse the film with reality. You think the ad should be withdrawn and that the company should publicly apologize for causing offence.

*Promotions Assistant*

You didn't like the ad. You thought it was over-dramatic. It painted a picture of a very frightening world. You agree with the Public Relations Manager that it was a mistake.

*Customer Service Manager*

You can't see what all the trouble is about. You found the ad very effective. The customers you have talked to don't seem to be offended. You think it is just the media blowing it up out of proportion.

# SPECIALIST AGENDA 7

## Finance

**ISSUE**

*You work for a limited company employing 150 workers. The company's main business is printing but it also has its own design studio. This month's regular finance committee meeting has a number of items on the agenda. For each item, use your own knowledge and the information under 'Roles'.*

**AGENDA**

1. **Valuing goodwill**
2. **Reductions in overhead costs**
3. **More transparent management accounts**
4. **Bank charges**

*Notes to the agenda*

1. *Valuing goodwill*

    Over the last two or three years, there have been one or two approaches from other bigger printing companies interested in buying your company. The Managing Director would like an approximate valuation of goodwill.

2. *Reductions in overhead costs*

    Suggestions for cutting overheads further would be welcome.

3. *More transparent management accounts*

    Some of the management have difficulty understanding the management accounts. How can they be made easier to read and interpret?

4. *Bank charges*

    Your annual turnover is £3.1 million. You pay £7,500 in bank charges every year. This covers all your costs of banking. Are there any ways to reduce these charges?

# Specialist Agenda 7

*Continued . . .*

---

## ROLES

### Finance Manager (Chair)

*Valuing goodwill:* This is very difficult to do. The easiest way is to take a percentage of the last five years' turnover.
*Reductions in overhead costs:* You are hoping that your staff will have analyzed the profit and loss account and come up with some suggestions.
*More transparent management accounts:* These are too complex. In your opinion, items should be grouped together for ease of understanding.
*Bank charges:* Your bank has offered to reduce their annual charge bill by 10 per cent. You feel you could get a better deal by changing to a new bank. This would have administrative costs etc.

### Chief Accountant

*Valuing goodwill:* There are formulae which can calculate goodwill. You offer to prepare some figures for the next meeting.
*Reductions in overhead costs:* Overheads have been steadily rising – particularly in the use of telephone and stationery. There needs to be more rigorous control in these areas.
*More transparent management accounts:* The best way is to just present sales, direct costs and overheads. If people require further detail, they can ask for it.
*Bank charges:* You don't want to change banks as this can cause problems with customers, suppliers etc. You think your present bank should offer a better deal.

### Chief Bookkeeper

*Valuing goodwill:* You don't have an opinion about this item.
*Reductions in overhead costs:* Analysis of itemized telephone bills shows that a lot of personal calls are made from the office. Telephone bills have risen by more than 10 per cent a year for the last three years, although charges have actually fallen.
*More transparent management accounts:* Managers are always coming to ask you for printouts of different nominal accounts. They should be trained to use the accounts software, on their own computers.
*Bank charges:* You have to deal with the bank every day. It is a disgrace that they charge so much money. They are very slow, inefficient and often unhelpful. You definitely think you should change banks.

### Financial Controller

*Valuing goodwill:* The company's goodwill value is really what the market will pay for the company over and above the asset value of the company. So you don't see why you should spend time trying to calculate it.
*Reductions in overhead costs:* Telephone costs have risen tremendously. Bills show that this is mainly due to more long-distance and international calls. The staff need to be made more aware of telephone charges and also the alternatives of fax and e-mail.
*More transparent management accounts:* All the managers should know more about the financial state of the company. Training in this area would be helpful.
*Bank charges:* Changing to a new bank in order to reduce charges might be a big mistake. Banks offer very attractive deals to persuade you to change and then slowly increase the charges over the following years. If the present service is not good enough, then that is a good reason to change.

# SPECIALIST AGENDA 8

## Legal affairs

**ISSUE**

*You work for a large international company. The legal department is mainly involved in drawing up contracts and advising on contractual and commercial law. The department meets every month to discuss current issues. Use your own knowledge and the points under 'Roles' to participate in the meeting*

**AGENDA**

1. Contract negotiations
2. Regional specialists
3. Insurance claims

*Notes to the agenda*

1. *Contract negotiations*

    Your company is involved in frequent international negotiations for large contracts overseas. The company's policy is for these negotiations to be carried out by someone from sales, a Technical Advisor and sometimes one of the Financial Managers. Members of the legal department are not present, although their advice is often needed.

2. *Regional specialists*

    The legal department is increasingly asked to deal with questions of law concerning specific parts of the world. Should the department employ more regional specialists or arrange co-operation with local legal firms?

3. *Insurance claims*

    The department is spending a lot of time processing trivial insurance claims, for example, for delayed travel, small thefts when travelling etc. Should the legal department be responsible for these claims?

# Specialist Agenda 8

*Continued . . .*

## ROLES

### Legal Affairs Manager (Chair)

*Contract negotiations:* One of your team should be present at negotiations, certainly for the final stages when the contracts are being discussed.
*Regional specialists:* The department cannot afford to hire permanent regional specialists but could try to establish links with local law firms.
*Insurance claims:* The legal department has to continue to process insurance claims. Too many mistakes are made otherwise and this just creates even more work.

### Legal Consultant 1

*Contract negotiations:* One of your team should be present throughout the negotiations. This could save a lot of time later when the contracts are drawn up.
*Regional specialists:* The company is doing a lot of business in South America and should employ someone who can speak Spanish, with a good knowledge of the law in that part of the world.
*Insurance claims:* The legal department should not have to deal with all these small claims. It is very time consuming and does not require legal expertise.

### Legal Consultant 2

*Contract negotiations:* It would be a waste of time for a lawyer to be present during these negotiations. Most of the time they are discussing terms and conditions i.e. price, delivery etc.; contracts are standard and can be prepared after the negotiation.
*Regional specialists:* The company should send legal staff on specialist legal training, for example contract law in South America. This would greatly improve the quality of advice.
*Insurance claims:* The legal department should not have to deal with all these small claims. It is very time consuming and does not require legal expertise.

### Legal Consultant 3

*Contract negotiations:* It would be helpful for a lawyer to be present at the end of the negotiations to draft the contract.
*Regional specialists:* The company should recruit from key areas in the world where the company is doing a lot of business.
*Insurance claims:* You have to deal with all the queries from insurance companies and this takes a lot of time. The department could assign this work to a clerk, rather than a fully qualified lawyer.

# SPECIALIST AGENDA 9

## Human resources (2)

**ISSUE**

*You work for a large- to medium-sized company employing around 1,450 people. Five people work in the human resources department. You meet regularly to discuss important issues. Use the information under 'Roles' and your own knowledge and experience to discuss the items below.*

**AGENDA**

1. **Jobsharing**
2. **Equal opportunities**
3. **Christmas party**

*Notes to the agenda*

1. *Jobsharing*

    There are two or three members of staff who would like to jobshare. Some managers are very against it, thinking that it will be more difficult to manage and could lead to inefficiency.

2. *Equal Opportunities*

    Despite the best efforts of the human resources department, there is only one woman who has reached a senior management position in the company. Should the company introduce positive discrimination when promoting staff in order to achieve a fairer balance?

3. *Christmas party*

    The Christmas party every year is held on the last afternoon/evening of work before Christmas. Some members of staff think that families of employees should also be invited to this party.

# Specialist Agenda 9

## Continued . . .

**ROLES**

*Human Resources Manager (Chair)*

*Jobsharing:* This can only work where two members of staff work in the same department and know the work well. In your experience people who jobshare do more than half a job. In this way, it is true that jobsharing is not very efficient.
*Equal opportunities:* You are not in favour of positive discrimination. You feel more women should be encouraged to apply for senior management positions.
*Christmas party:* You are not in favour of asking families to the Christmas party. For you the Christmas party is an opportunity just for colleagues to celebrate the end of the year.

*Personnel Officer 1*

*Jobsharing:* This is a good idea, especially for parents who have children at home. You think the company should support this arrangement for members of staff who would like to work this way.
*Equal opportunities:* You are not in favour of positive discrimination for women. However, you feel male managers should be encouraged to appoint women to more senior positions.
*Christmas party:* You are in favour of asking families to the Christmas party. It would be a good opportunity for staff and families to meet each other.

*Personnel Officer 2*

*Jobsharing:* This is not a good idea. It would lead to duplication of work and that it would be difficult for other members of staff to have to communicate with two people rather than one person.
*Equal opportunities:* You are not in favour of positive discrimination for women. However, you feel male managers should be encouraged to appoint women to more senior positions.
*Christmas party:* You are not in favour of asking families to the Christmas party. It is the only occasion in the year when colleagues get together informally. It would be a mistake to include partners and children.

*Personnel Officer 3*

*Jobsharing:* This is a good idea. It would lead to more flexibility at work and probably more dynamism from two people rather than one.
*Equal opportunities:* You are not in favour of positive discrimination for women. However, you think the company should do some training in this area to encourage women to be more assertive.
*Christmas party:* you are in favour of asking families to the Christmas party. It is the only occasion in the year when colleagues get together informally. It would be nice to invite family as well.

*Personnel Officer 4*

*Jobsharing:* This is a good idea. It would lead to more flexibility at work and it would help those members of staff who don't want to or can't work full-time.
*Equal opportunities:* The only way to increase the number of women in top management jobs is to discriminate in favour of them. After all, that is what has happened for men for the last 100 years.
*Christmas party:* You are in favour of asking families to the Christmas party. It is the only occasion in the year when colleagues get together informally. It would be nice to invite family as well.

# SPECIALIST AGENDA 10

## Production

**ISSUE**

*Your company employs about 1000 people mainly involved in the production of electronic components. In the production department, there are four managers/supervisors who meet regularly to discuss problems and issues. Use your own experience and knowledge, plus the 'Roles', to discuss the items below.*

**AGENDA**

    1  Rest times

    2  Apprentices

    3  Safety training

*Notes to the agenda*

    1  *Rest-times*

        The factory used to have three breaks a shift: two 15-minute and one 30-minute break.

        Production planning would be easier if there were two 30-minute breaks in an 8 hour shift. Many production workers are unhappy about this suggested change.

    2  *Apprentices*

        You have reduced the number of young apprentices that you employ each year. As a result, there is a much faster turnover of workers in the factory; they don't stay for so long. Employing apprentices is one way to ensure expertise stays in the company in the long term.

    3  *Safety training*

        Safety training is carried out regularly for all factory workers. The company would like to encourage more workers to become 'first-aiders' (qualified to give first aid in an emergency). The meeting needs to decide whether it will finance people to attend the necessary course.

# Specialist Agenda 10

## Continued . . .

**ROLES**

*Production Manager (Chair)*

*Rest times:* Two breaks a shift is far easier to plan in terms of staffing the machines. A total of 60 minutes break time a shift is very generous and the workers have no reason for complaining.
*Apprentices:* You would like to hire more apprentices but the company policy is not to give long-term contracts. You feel this is short-sighted and would like to persuade the board to change their minds.
*Safety training:* You feel the company should pay for workers to attend the first-aid evening classes.

*Shift supervisor 1*

*Rest times:* The workers would be happier with three 15-minute breaks rather than two 30-minute breaks. This would save 15 minutes in rest time. The work is monotonous and you need regular breaks.
*Apprentices:* The solution to the rapid employee turnover is to provide more training and promotion opportunities for the production line workers. You don't think hiring more apprentices is the answer.
*Safety training:* The company should pay for workers to attend the first-aid evening classes and also provide a salary incentive for getting the qualification.

*Shift supervisor 2*

*Rest times:* The existing break system is best. Workers need 30 minutes in the middle of the shift to have something to eat, and 15-minute breaks to have a coffee, go to the rest rooms, etc.
*Apprentices:* You like the idea of hiring more apprentices. It would help the youth unemployment problem in the local community. Also, it would be good to have some young people in the factory.
*Safety training:* The company should pay for workers to attend the first-aid evening classes.

*Shift supervisor 3*

*Rest times:* The suggested new system will be fine. Nobody likes change but it is just a question of getting used to it.
*Apprentices:* You don't think young people are interested in becoming apprentices any more. Staff turnover would be improved if the salaries became more competitive.
*Safety training:* You feel the company should pay for workers to attend the first-aid evening classes.

# DECISION-MAKING 1

## Outsourcing or not?

**ISSUE**

*Your company has had a department looking after its information technology needs for 20 years. It was called the computer department, then EDP (electronic data processing) and now IT (information technology) but basically it has done the same job: making sure that the IT services run smoothly throughout the company. The company employs six people:*

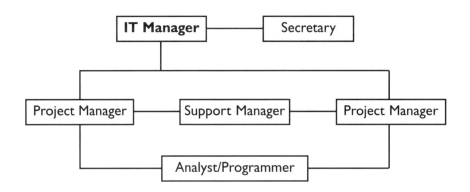

*The annual investment budget for IT is around £150,000. The maintenance budget which covers repairs, spare parts and replacements is £120,000. The total payroll bill for the department is £155,000. Therefore the total IT budget is £425,000.*

*You have received three tenders to take over the IT services. They all will cost considerably less, ranging from £220,000 to £380,000. They are all reputable IT support companies.*

**AGENDA**

1 Information Technology Manager: the argument against outsourcing.
2 Finance Manager: the argument in favour.
3 Discussion and decision.

# Decision-making 1

## Continued . . .

**ROLES**

### Managing Director (Chair)

You are not yet convinced of the sense of subcontracting information technology. You have a certain amount of loyalty to the in-house team and they have done a good job. However, your first responsibility is to ensure the profitability of the business and the IT budget seems to have got out of control.

### The Computer Manager

You are fighting for your team's survival. You need to talk about the plus points:
1 You know the company
2 You are permanently on-site
3 Your team presents no security hazard
4 Information technology know-how is an area of expertise which the company needs to have

as well as the risks of outsourcing:
1 Delays in support
2 Security risks
3 Losing the expertise.

### Finance Manager

You feel there is no option but to outsource this work. The present budget of nearly half a million is much too high, given that this is not central to your business.

### Computer Project Manager

You are currently working on a project to upgrade all the desktop computers. You think it would create chaos if this type of work was suddenly taken over by an outside contractor. You know the staff, you know their problems, you can fit round their jobs, etc.

### Customer Service Manager

You use the IT services extensively. You are very happy with the work they do. It is absolutely vital. On the other hand, you were shocked to hear about their total annual budget. Can't they make some cuts?

### Sales Manager

Your salesmen use the IT system a lot. You also feel the IT department does a very difficult job well. You don't like the idea of outside contractors having access to potentially very confidential information.

# DECISION-MAKING 2

## New training manager

**ISSUE**

*Your company has decided to hire a training manager. Previously this area has been looked after by the Human Resources Manager. You have a short list of four candidates. You need to decide which one to choose.*

**AGENDA**

    1  Presentation of candidates by the Human Resources Manager

    2  Discussion

    3  Decision

**ROLES**

Expand on your views based on the information under 'Candidate'.

*Human Resources Manager*

You should present the candidates. You have no preference.

*Sales Manager*

You were on the interview panel. You liked Linda McEwan. Argue the case for her.

*Production Manager*

You were on the interview panel. You liked Donald Brennan. Argue the case for him.

*Marketing Manager*

You were on the interview panel. You liked Terry Brown. Argue the case for him.

*Personnel Assistant*

You were on the interview panel. You liked Diane Sonley. Argue the case for her.

# Decision-making 2

## *Continued . . .*

**CANDIDATES**

*Terry Brown*

*Personal:* Age: 35, married with two children. Interests: rock music and squash
*Professional:* MBA, Member of ITD.
    Personnel Officer: Court Holdings
    Training Manager: Court Holdings
    Management Development Co-ordinator: Sovereign PLC
Very personable, easy-going. Perhaps lacks dynamism. Good training professional but rather limited experience. Good team player, maybe not leader.

*Diane Sonley*

*Personal:* Age: 29, single. Interests: mountaineering, theatre
*Professional:* BA History, Diploma in Personnel Management
    Training Officer: BAT Industries
    Training Manager: Scottish Life Insurance
    Training Manager: Amersham International
Quite serious. Conscientious. Very professional. Ambitious. Would push training hard but might clash with some other managers.

*Linda McEwan*

*Personal:* Age: 39, divorced, three children. Interests: reading, politics, art
*Professional:* BA English and Philosophy, PhD Philosophy
    Research Assistant: Edinburgh University
    Lecturer: Edinburgh University
    Training and Development Manager: Stirling College
    Training Manager: Amoco North Sea Operations
    Training Manager: Unicorn Oil, Aberdeen
Very interesting candidate. Has worked in training for 5 years. Previously an academic. Very well informed, intelligent. Perhaps too bright for the job. Would she stay?

*Donald Brennan*

*Personal:* Age: 41, married, no children. Interests: archaeology, travel
*Professional:* Certificate in Teaching, MA in Education
    Teacher: Norwich Secondary School
    Head of Arts Dept: Norwich Secondary School
    Deputy Head: Norwich Secondary School
    Training Advisor: Norfolk County Council
    Training Manager: Norley Institute
He was made redundant from Norwich Secondary School four years ago. Since then he has been working in training. A very good teacher, excellent with people. No real management experience but probably quick to learn.

# DECISION-MAKING 3

## The budget

**ISSUE**

It is half way through your financial year. Sales are running about 5 per cent below target and as a result, overheads have to be cut. The Financial Manager has called this meeting to agree budget cuts with five department heads.

| Department | year to date spending | budget | annual budget | revised budget |
|---|---|---|---|---|
| Marketing | $145,000 | 143,000 | 290,000 | 260,000 |
| Administration | $340,000 | 350,000 | 700,000 | 625,000 |
| Personnel | $105,000 | 100,000 | 200,000 | 180,000 |
| Training | $85,000 | 82,000 | 164,000 | 140,000 |
| IT Support | $195,000 | 150,000 | 300,000 | 250,000 |
| Totals | | | 1,654,000 | 1,455,000 |

**AGENDA**

1 Need for budget cuts
2 Response of department heads to proposed cuts
3 Revised budget allocation

*Notes to the agenda*

1 *Need for Budget cuts*
   The Finance Manager will present the reasons for the cuts.

2 *Response of department heads to proposed cuts*
   The department heads will present the responses to the cuts. Discussion of each case.

3 *Revised budget allocation*
   Final decision about how to make an overall 10 per cent cut.

# Decision-making 3

*Continued . . .*

## ROLES

### Finance Manager

Your job is to make sure that the budget has been cut by 10 per cent overall at the end of the meeting. You know that there will be a lot of resistance from all the department heads.

### Marketing Manager

If the proposed budget cut of $30,000 goes through, you will have to cancel at least three marketing projects. All current projects are designed to support sales and boost the image of the company. You could reduce your budget by maybe $15,000 by cancelling a project planned for the last quarter. This sales promotion event could be postponed to the following year.

### Administration Manager

The proposed $75,000 cut in your budget would be disastrous. All your budget has been allocated to staff salaries, administrative systems etc. The only possible cut could be in the area of refurbishment. You are half way through redecorating and refurnishing the offices. You could stop this process and save around $50,000. It would mean some people have nice new offices and others don't.

### Personnel Manager

Like the Administration Manager you have no special projects you can cut. Your whole budget has been allocated to staff costs and personnel support. The only way you can reduce by $20,000 is by losing one, maybe two members of staff.

### Training Manager

The proposed $24,000 cut in your budget would be very bad for the company. It would mean cancelling several training programmes planned for the second half of the year. This would be bad for morale and personnel development. The only cut you could make is to run two courses in-house, rather than in a hotel; this would reduce the costs by $8,000.

### IT Support

The proposed $50,000 budget cut seems totally wrong to you. It is considerably more than 10 per cent and IT is essential to the company. This sort of cut could only be achieved by losing at least two members of staff. You could reduce the budget by about £20,000 if you delay the introduction of some new desktop systems.

# PROBLEM-SOLVING 1

## Time management

**ISSUE**

*You recently carried out a survey of how managers in your company spend their time. Here are the results:*

| | |
|---|---|
| Travelling: | 10 per cent |
| Meetings: | 35 per cent |
| Writing: | 10 per cent |
| Thinking: | 5 per cent |
| Reading: | 10 per cent |
| Talking: | 30 per cent |

*All of the managers felt they spent too much time in meetings, not enough time managing people and work on a day to day basis.*

*Your task is to reduce time in meetings.*

**AGENDA**

1. What are we doing in meetings?
2. How can we make meetings shorter?
3. How can we reduce the number of meetings?
4. Action plan

# Problem-solving 1

## Continued...

**ROLES**

### Manager 1

You hate meetings. You think they should be cut drastically. You think that the answer is to use electronic mail to keep people informed and only have meetings for decisions.

### Manager 2

You don't like meetings. However you feel they are a necessary evil to keep people working as a team. You think most meetings could be better chaired.

### Manager 3

You think the meetings are fine as they are. You feel they are effective in keeping everybody up to date and involved.

### Manager 4

You think the meetings could be improved. Better chairing, tighter time-keeping and restriction of the agenda to essential items.

**ADDITIONAL ROLES: USE PERSONAL OPINIONS.**

# PROBLEM-SOLVING 2

## Staff morale

**ISSUE**

You have carried out a survey at work and found that staff morale is low:

| | |
|---|---|
| I enjoy coming to work | 27 per cent |
| I don't mind coming to work | 26 per cent |
| I would prefer to stay at home | 24 per cent |
| I hate coming to work | 23 per cent |

*Reasons I don't get job satisfaction*

| | |
|---|---|
| Pay is too low | 10 per cent |
| Job is too routine | 35 per cent |
| Atmosphere is not friendly | 25 per cent |
| Job is too difficult | 15 per cent |
| Hours are too long | 15 per cent |

Your task is to improve staff morale. Below are some suggestions to start the discussion.

- *Better job descriptions*
- *Introduce a performance appraisal system*
- *Start a staff social club*
- *Start a programme of team-building courses*
- *Introduce profit sharing*

**AGENDA**

1. **Survey results**
2. **Improving staff morale**
3. **Action plan**

*Notes to the agenda*

1. *Survey results*
   Brief discussion of results and reasons
2. *Improving staff morale*
   Brainstorming on different ways to improve morale
3. *Action plan*
   Decisions about what action to take.

# Problem-solving 2

## Continued . . .

**ROLES**

### Manager 1

You think staff morale is low because everybody is overworked. The answer is to recruit more people and reduce working hours.

### Manager 2

You think staff morale is low because some of the managers are too authoritarian. You feel the atmosphere would be improved at work if team spirit was bettter.

### Manager 3

You think staff morale is low because staff have been in their jobs too long, They need to have a change. You think job rotation could be the answer.

### Manager 4

You think staff morale is low because many of the jobs are repetitive. You think you need to create better social facilities to compensate for this.

### Manager 5

You think staff morale is low because of low pay. The only answer is to substantially increase salaries.

# PROBLEM-SOLVING 3

## Personality clash

**ISSUE**

*Peter Matthews, a technical representative, joined your company 3 years ago. He is very good at the technical part of his job. Unfortunately he is not at all easy to work with. He tends to be rather distant and even arrogant. He doesn't mix with his colleagues and can be rude on occasions. He has already been moved twice to different departments. His colleagues are complaining that they cannot work with him. What can you do about him?*

*Your task is to come up with some concrete suggestions.*

**AGENDA**

1. **The problem**
2. **Possible solutions**
3. **Action**

*Notes to the agenda*

1. *The problem*
   Clarify exactly what the problem is.
2. *Possible solutions*
   Brainstorm possible solutions (e.g. training, transfer, promotion, demotion, etc.).
3. *Action*
   Decide on a course of action.

# Problem-solving 3

*Continued . . .*

**ROLES**

*Manager 1*

You think the only answer is to get rid of Peter. You feel he is never going to fit in.

*Manager 2*

You think the company should be able to accommodate different types. You think some training in interpersonal skills should help Peter.

*Manager 3*

You think Peter should be transferred to another part of the company where he can work on his own.

*Manager 4*

You think Peter should be offered more training and, if this doesn't succeed, fired.

*Manager 5*

You think Peter should be moved to another department.

# PROBLEM-SOLVING 4

## Working time and lunch-time

**ISSUE**

You operate a 35-hour working week for all white collar workers. As no specific time has been set aside for lunch and there is no canteen, the staff have traditionally taken around 60 minutes some time between 12.30 and 14.00. During this time they have usually gone out to take a break from the office. You have recently noticed that more and more of the staff are not taking a lunch break and are eating their lunch in the office over their computers. In addition, you have noticed that there have been a number of spillages of drinks over the computers in the last few months. This has caused some inconvenience as keyboards have had to be cleaned, and on one occasion a computer's hard disk had to be replaced. However, you are aware that the clerical staff are often under pressure to finish work, especially at the end of the week, so that all the data has been input in time for the end-of-week processing.

Your task is to decide a policy:

- for lunch break
- for the consumption of food and drink near the computers.

**AGENDA**

1. Presentation of the problem
2. Is a lunch break necessary and if so, how long?
3. Policy on eating/drinking:
   - in the office
   - near computers
4. How to communicate this to the staff
5. Action plan

*Notes to the agenda*

1. *The problem*
   Clarify exactly what the problem is.
2. *Possible solutions*
   Brainstorm alternatives and make a decision on the most appropriate one.
3. *Policy on eating/drinking near computers*
   Brainstorm alternatives and make a decision on the most appropriate one.
4. *Action plan*
   Decide on a course of action.

# Problem-solving 4

## *Continued . . .*

**ROLES**

*Managing Director*

You believe that staff should take a 60-minute break for lunch and should, ideally, leave their offices for a change of environment.

*Administration Manager*

You believe that the policy should be flexible. When there is a lot of work to do, the staff need to put in extra hours. Rather than having them stay late in the evenings, it is better for them to work at lunch time.

*Marketing Manager*

As you are often out with clients in the mornings and the afternoons, the lunch break is the only time when you can get into the office. You find it useful that the admin (administration) staff are at their desks, because you can ask them to type up proposals for you.

*Finance Manager*

The recent bills for equipment repairs have worried you. You would like to see a ban on all food and drink in the offices.

*Staff Representative*

You believe that the current practice of shorter lunch breaks is good for morale. Your staff can get home earlier and this suits them. It also suits the company that work can be completed more quickly.

*Information Technology Manager*

It is an agreed rule among computer users that no food or drink should be kept near machines. It is dangerous for the users and potentially damaging to the equipment.

# PROBLEM-SOLVING 5

## Use of the Internet

**ISSUE**

*Your staff in your company's research department regularly use the Internet to search for business leads, who are then e-mailed to offer your services. However, you have noted a steady increase in the telecommunications bill. This is not unexpected with the use of the Internet. However, you have seen that some of the staff are surfing the Internet for their own personal use – to find information about cheap offers, especially holidays, and even to do their shopping. On the one hand, this is not part of their job; on the other, it shows their interest in the Internet as a marketing tool and has thrown up some useful business leads for the company.*

*Up to now, it has been your company's unwritten policy to allow staff to make local calls from their phones, as these have usually been short calls to family or to make arrangements for appointments to the doctor, dentist, etc. Your Internet provider has a local number, so all calls are charged at local rates.*

*Your task is to decide on a policy on Internet use and the method to implement it.*

**AGENDA**

1. Presentation of the problem
2. Review of the policy on the use of the phone for personal calls
3. Policy on the use of the Internet for personal purposes
4. How to implement policy decisions
5. Action plan

*Notes to the agenda*

1. *The problem*
   Clarify exactly what the problem is.
2. *Possible solutions*
   Brainstorm possible solutions.
3. *Action plan*
   Decide on a course of action.

# Problem-solving 5

## Continued...

**ROLES**

### Managing Director

You are not very technologically minded. When asked whether the staff could use the Internet for local calls you agreed. You think it is a small gesture to the staff for their hard work.

### Finance Manager

At the beginning, the use of the Internet was limited and the phone bills small. In recent months the bill has grown. You believe that it could become a major cost if something isn't done now to stop private use.

### Marketing Manager

You have been impressed by the quality of the research done by the Internet group. In fact, they often find useful business contacts on their own initiative. These have led to new business that you hadn't expected. Therefore, you would like to encourage them to make more use of the Internet. It's good for company business.

### Staff Representative

Internet is an enjoyable tool to work with. It is certainly more fun than reading through trade magazines to find possible contacts. You are very pleased that the company is using the new technology. If they allowed private calls before, you can't see why there is such a fuss now.

### Administration Manager

You feel that the use of Internet for personal shopping is a passing phase. Soon the attraction will wear off and the staff will return to their normal use of the phone for private purposes.

### Information Technology Manager

You have access to the Internet sites that the staff visit. You know that they not only surf the net to find bargains but they also visit some of the chat line and sex line sites. You feel that personal shopping is justified, but visiting other sites should not be at the company's expense.

# PROBLEM-SOLVING 6

## Poaching

**ISSUE**

*Friendly rivalry between you and Manson Industries has been going on for years. However, last year, when your Finance Director was poached by Manson, you felt that your competitor had acted in an underhand manner. The subsequent financial restructuring of Manson showed that the new recruit had also provided Manson with sensitive financial information.*

*Your own policy was 'business as usual' and you subsequently filled the vacant post by an internal promotion from the finance department. You are now seeking to appoint or recruit a Marketing and Sales Director and the best candidate supplied to you by the head-hunting agency is at present employed by Manson Industries. If he is the best candidate, you would certainly want to appoint him. In addition, it would be very tempting to get market information from him in order to compete more effectively with Manson.*

*Your task is to decide on an appropriate policy in general and what to do in this particular situation.*

**AGENDA**

1. Presentation of the problem
2. Outline of the available options
3. Decision on action to be taken
4. Action plan

*Notes to the agenda*

1. *The problem*
   Clarify exactly what the problem is.
2. *Possible solutions*
   Brainstorm alternative courses of action and make a decision on the most appropriate one.
3. *Policy decision*
   Decide on an appropriate policy for the company.
4. *Action plan*
   Decide on a course of action to implement the decisions.

# Problem-solving 6

## Continued . . .

## ROLES

### Human Resources Director

One of your roles as Human Resources Director is to fill company posts with the best candidates. Therefore, you would like to appoint the candidate from Manson Industries.

### Managing Director

You have steered the company through a number of difficult years. Although Manson is a competitor, you have learned from experience that is better to avoid possible scandals. And, more importantly, to keep issues like poaching out of the news.

### Marketing Manager

You have been promoted to Managing Director at one of the company's subsidiaries. You are keen to see an able replacement, with good local and product knowledge. The Manson candidate has exactly the right profile. He would also bring with him market information about Manson which could be very useful throughout the company.

### Finance Director

When the previous Finance Director was poached by Manson, you were promoted internally to your present position. In fact, you were grateful to Manson for giving you such a good opportunity. On the other hand, you know that your predecessor gave sensitive financial information to Manson. This has caused a number of problems in your job.

### Legal Manager

Poaching causes more problems than it is worth. Although there are no technical reasons why you should not take on the Manson candidate, you believe that it would set a good example to other companies if you behaved ethically and gave the job to another candidate.

### Sales Manager

You know the prospective candidate and don't like him. He has an impressive track record, but is ruthless and self-centred. You would not like to work under him. In fact, if he was appointed you would probably leave.

# PROBLEM-SOLVING 7

## Delegation

**ISSUE**

You have recently been appointed as Junior Manager and are keen to do the job well. Last week you delegated a routine task (preparing and sending out some marketing literature with a covering letter) to a subordinate, whom you felt sure could manage the job. You have now received some feedback from clients who have said that:

- the material was sent to the wrong person in the organization
- the covering letter contained inaccurate information
- product names were misspelt.

As a result, you now feel very bad about delegating the task.

Your task is to prepare guidelines for delegation.

**AGENDA**

1. What can be delegated?
2. When can tasks be delegated?
3. How should delegation be handled and monitored?
4. Action plan

*Notes to the agenda*

1. *The problem*
   Clarify exactly what the problem is.
2. *Possible solutions*
   Brainstorm parameters for effective delegation.
3. *Action plan*
   Draw up recommendations for effective delegation within the company.

# Problem-solving 7

## Continued . . .

## ROLES

### Managing Director

You believe that delegation is one of the key skills that every manager must have. You must know what to delegate and how to delegate.

### Human Resources Director

Delegation is a very important skill. Unfortunately, most managers don't know how to delegate. They simply give tasks to subordinates without explaining exactly what is required. Then they are surprised when things go wrong.

### Junior Manager

You thought you had done everything correctly. You believed you had chosen the right person and talked through what you wanted.

### Sales Manager

You work with a team of 20 sales representatives. You know that building a team requires effort, patience and a lot of dedication. It's the same with delegation. One must gain people's trust before one can delegate effectively.

### Finance Manager

Teamwork is overrated. If you want something doing, either you do it yourself or you give someone you trust very specific orders. If it goes wrong, you tell the person to do it again, until they get it right.

### Staff Representative

You feel that the company is full of managers who are looking for subordinates to do their jobs for them. Delegation is simply a way of handing round the work so that others have to take responsibility when things go wrong.

# PROBLEM-SOLVING 8

## Open-plan

**ISSUE**

As Facilities Manager, you have been given the responsibility of collecting ideas for the redesign of your company's head office. The current restructuring means that you will need to accommodate 250 staff in a building which currently provides office space for 150. The present arrangement consists of individual offices, occupied either by one person or a small team. The preliminary results of your survey show:

- the present arrangement is uneconomic in terms of space utilization
- many managers are against the idea of open-plan offices
- some of the company's managers work on outside contracts, and, as a result individual offices are often empty for days or even weeks.

Your task is to decide on the redesign of the work space. Some alternatives are:

- an open-plan office or a number of open-plan offices
- shared desks for managers who spend more than 30 per cent of their work time off-site.

**AGENDA**

1. **Presentation of the problem and preliminary results**
2. **Discussion of alternatives**
3. **Decision on next step**
4. **Action plan**

*Notes to the agenda*

1. *The problem*
   Clarify exactly what the problem is and the results of the survey.
2. *Possible solutions*
   Brainstorm possible alternatives.
3. *Decision*
   Decide on the best alternatives.
4. *Action plan*
   Decide on a course of action to implement the decisions.

# Problem-solving 8

*Continued . . .*

---

## ROLES

### Facilities Manager (Chair)

You recently joined the company and this is your first opportunity to work on a major project. You would like to impress your colleagues with your radical plan to change how and where the company works. You would like to see the work space with open-plan and shared desks.

### Managing Director

You are five years away from retirement. As the company is in a fair financial state, you don't want a major change to current working practices. This could lead to the departure of the some of the directors. You would, therefore, like minimum disruption.

### Administration Manager

You like the idea of open-plan working. It would make it easier for you to have contact with the administrative staff. This would improve team working and, in turn, efficiency.

### Marketing Director

You can see the reasons for sharing desks, but you can't see how it would work in practice. In any case, your sales team would be very unhappy to lose their own desks. It could also lead to problems of security, if others had access to information.

### Finance Manager

You would like to see a cost-effective solution. The buildings are in need of major renovation. It would, therefore, make sense to use the opportunity to upgrade the facilities to accommodate the extra numbers.

### Staff Representative

You are concerned about the extra staff working in the same building. The present building is already quite full. Another 100 people would make it very difficult to work. As there is an empty building less than 250 metres away, you think that the company should acquire that and operate from two sites.

# PROBLEM-SOLVING 9

## Training course vs. on-the-job training

**ISSUE**

Your company has recently appointed a new training manager who has introduced a new programme of leadership and training activities for executives. Some of these are in-house programmes and some out-house, involving participation with other companies.

You were recently persuaded to join an encounter weekend training programme for executives. The programme was organized for 12 participants from different local companies. The weekend was organized by an external company, made up of ex-army personnel. It turned out to be a nightmare of challenging tasks in difficult conditions, ostensibly to teach leadership and team skills. After the course you were totally exhausted and needed a week to recover. As a result, you feel that the same skills could have been learned:

- through a less painful experience
- together with people from the same organization
- in a less threatening situation.

The company now proposes to send two more young managers on a leadership course. Your task is to decide whether this type of training programme is appropriate for your company's needs.

**AGENDA**

1. What are leadership skills?
2. What tasks develop leadership skills?
3. What types of training programmes can develop these skills?
4. What programmes are suitable for different grades of manager/directors?
5. Action plan

*Notes to the agenda*

1. *The problem*
   Clarify exactly what the problem is.
2. *Leadership and how to develop it*
   Brainstorm:
   - what is leadership
   - how to develop it.
3. *Leadership in the company*
   Discuss alternative methods to develop leadership skills within the company.
4. *Action plan*
   Decide on a course of action to implement the decisions.

# Problem-solving 9

## Continued . . .

**ROLES**

*Finance Manager and former trainee*

You see the benefits of leadership training and feel that the company needs more of it. However, the leadership weekend was a painful experience and you feel that the results did not justify the means.

*Managing Director*

You are an ex-army officer. You believe that a little hardship is good for today's managers. It helps them to develop and this is good for the company.

*Human Resources Director*

You reluctantly agreed to send the Finance Manager on the leadership training course. You believed he was the wrong person for this type of programme. These types of training programme are only useful with the right individual. If you send the wrong person, it can leave lasting damage.

*Administration Manager*

You believe that the company does not offer enough training. At annual meetings, the Training Manager always promises more training, but when you ask for programmes, you are always told to wait. You support the Training Manager's action because it was at least a new initiative.

*Sales Manager*

You believe that on-the-job training is the only way to develop the right skills. You have trained all your salesmen yourself and they are doing an excellent job.

*Training Manager*

You believe the company needs new training ideas – both on-the-job and off-the-job. You thought that the course was right for the Finance Manager. In any case, he said he wanted a challenge.

# PROBLEM-SOLVING 10

## Employment of disabled people

**ISSUE**

*A government scheme has recently been introduced to encourage companies to employ disabled people. The encouragement comes in the form of financial subsidies for each disabled person taken on. Your company would pay 50 per cent of the wage and the government would match this.*

*Your company employs 150 people in the manufacture of circuit boards. Much of the production itself requires specialist skills, though the packaging and loading does not.*

*Your task is to decide whether it is appropriate to employ disabled people.*

**AGENDA**

1. The principle of employing disabled people
2. The practical aspects of identifying suitable jobs
3. The effect on other employees
4. Steps to integrate disabled people smoothly into the company
5. Action plan

*Notes to the agenda*

1. *The issue*
   Clarify exactly what the issue is.
2. *Possible solutions*
   Brainstorm alternative courses of action and make a decision on the most appropriate one.
3. *Policy decision*
   Decide on the appropriate policy for the company.
4. *Action plan*
   Decide on a course of action to implement the decision(s).

# Problem-solving 10

## Continued . . .

**ROLES**

*Production Director*

The production of circuit board requires specialist skills. Therefore, you feel it would be difficult to find suitable jobs for disabled people. You think it would be a false economy.

*Marketing Director*

Employing disabled people would be good for the profile of company. It would show you as a 'caring employer'.

*Administration Manager*

You used to work in a company which employed disabled people. They needed a lot of extra attention. You are already stretched in your job. If you had to look after the needs of more people, it would make your job more difficult.

*Human Resources Director*

Employing disabled people would be good for links with the community. This is an initiative you are keen to develop.

*Finance Manager*

The financial equation is clear. Employing disabled people would keep costs down. It would also allow the company to expand without a major increase in the payroll.

*Staff Representative*

You believe it would reduce jobs for existing staff and could lead to layoffs and redundancies. You need to protect the interests of your colleagues. Therefore, you are against it.

# PROBLEM-SOLVING 11

## Recycling

**ISSUE**

*As an environmentally conscious company you regularly recycle paper, glass and tins. The offices all have separate bins for different types of garbage and the office cleaners make sure that the rubbish is put into separate containers for collection by a private garbage collection and recycling company, which you have to pay for. On the other hand, the local rubbish collection service, which you don't use, because it doesn't recycle waste, is already paid for out of your business taxes.*

*The private collection company have recently informed you that due to a glut of garbage and the high cost of recycling, they will have to increase their prices by 25 per cent next year.*

*Your task is to decide what to do with the rubbish.*

**AGENDA**

1 Presentation of the problem
2 Discussion of alternatives
3 Decision on next step
4 Action plan

*Notes to the agenda*

1 *The problem*
   Clarify exactly what the problem is.
2 *Possible solutions*
   Brainstorm alternative courses of action and make a decision on the most appropriate one.
3 *Policy decision*
   Decide on an appropriate policy for the company.
4 *Action plan*
   Decide on a course of action to implement the decisions.

# Problem-solving 11

## Continued...

**ROLES**

*Facilities Manager*

You introduced the agreement with the private company. At that time you had the support of the management team. Now that support is wavering. The main reason is that the private company is involved in recycling nuclear waste.

*Administration Manager*

You favour extending the agreement with the present private company. You believe that the environmental benefits justify the higher price.

*Marketing Manager*

The environment is a good marketing issue at the moment. The messages which show that you are an environmentally-friendly company help to boost sales. You believe that you should continue with the private company.

*Finance Manager*

When there was only a small price differential between the local rubbish service and the private service, you agreed to hire the private company. Now they are much more expensive. You can't see the benefit in paying extra money for the same service.

*Staff Representative*

The company has become more environmentally-conscious in recent years. You have done a lot to introduce environmental issues into the agenda. These include separate bins for rubbish, switching off the lights when not in use and more vegetarian food on the canteen menu. You believe that these initiatives are good for the company and give the staff a set of values in a very consumerist world. You think that the continued use of the private company is a good investment.

*Managing Director*

You think that the increased environmental awareness of the staff is taking their minds off the main purpose, which is to make money for the shareholders.

# PROBLEM-SOLVING 12

## An attractive remuneration package

**ISSUE**

As the state pays less and less in old age pension, it is becoming increasingly important for those who want to enjoy their 'golden years' to have their own private pension arrangements. In order to satisfy the growing need for private pension arrangements, you and your colleagues have recently set up your own company to offer a range of financial services and products. Your target market is small- and medium-sized companies, in which the directors have not made sufficient arrangements for their own pensions.

The services that you will offer are:

- pension audit (to identify the pension required)
- pension advice (to look at present pension provision and identify possible alternative providers)
- pension products (to sell pension schemes).

As you and your colleagues spend a great deal of your time out of the office with clients, you need an assistant to manage the office in your absence. You envisage that this will be a key position (more than simply an administrative job), as the person recruited will have a lot of customer contact, often giving advice and even selling products.

You need to agree on a remuneration package that will attract the right person.

**AGENDA**

1. Presentation of the problem
2. Discussion of alternatives
3. Decision on next step
4. Action plan

*Notes to the agenda*

1. *The problem*
   Clarify exactly what the problem is.
2. *Possible solutions*
   Brainstorm alternative courses of action and make a decision on the most appropriate one.
3. *Policy decision*
   Decide on an appropriate policy for the company.
4. *Action plan*
   Decide on a course of action to implement the decisions.

# Problem-solving 12

## Continued . . .

**ROLES**

*Partner 1*

You can't afford to pay a high salary at the moment. So, you favour a scheme which gives the person recruited a small share in the company's profits.

*Partner 2*

You believe you should offer an attractive salary in order to get the right person. You know it will be difficult to cover the costs, but you believe it will pay for itself once the right person is installed.

*Partner 3*

You know there are a lot of people looking for jobs. Many of them, especially women returning to work after bringing up a family, are well qualified and not very expensive. You think that the key is to recruit someone who has been out of the work market for some years, and train him or her. That would keep costs down.

*Partner 4*

You believe that the right work environment is more important than money. This means opportunities for personal and professional development.

*Partner 5*

You believe that a pay package linked to the success of the company will attract the right person. You favour an annual bonus based on the company's profits.

*Partner 6*

You believe that it is important to recruit for the long term. If you pay a low rate, then the person may leave when he or she finds a better job. You need someone who will stay with the company, and money is an important factor in getting long-term commitment.

# STRATEGY MEETING 1

## Mission statement

**ISSUE**

*A mission statement is a statement of the aims, purposes and future activities of an organization. The objective of the mission statement is to define for the company's stakeholders – its company's employees, customers and shareholders – what kind of organization it is, what it believes in and in which direction it wants to go.*

*Here is an example of the mission statement of an international pharmaceutical company:*

> We aim to be the preferred supplier of pharmaceutical products in the United States and selected international markets, achieving the long-term growth and financial performance of a market leader.
>
> The critical factors that drive our success are:
> - customer focus
> - wide product range
> - continuous process and product improvement
> - short lead times from development to market
> - reduced production costs
> - total quality environment
> - high standards of integrity and ethical conduct.

*Now write a mission statement for a real or imaginary service company. First choose or invent the company and its service sector. Then write the text for the statement.*

**AGENDA**

1. The aims of the mission statement
2. The content of the mission statement
3. The wording of the mission statement

*Notes to the agenda*

1. Each director will present their views on the three items on the agenda.
2. Each director will use the relevant section from 'Roles and Contributions' to play their part in the discussion which will then agree a text for the final document.
3. The team will draft the final document.

# Strategy Meeting 1

*Continued . . .*

## ROLES AND CONTRIBUTIONS

### Managing Director

You believe that the mission statement should include wording about the higher ideals of the company. You know that, in the business world, there are many directors who misuse their positions and status. You believe that the stakeholders need to see that your company behaves ethically.

### Marketing Director

You are concerned with products and the markets for your products. You believe that the stakeholders need to see that your company is successful in those areas. Therefore, you think that the mission statement should include wording about the customer focus and your wide product range.

### Human Resources Director

After a period of streamlining and downsizing, your company is now leaner and slimmer. There have been many redundancies. It is now time to show the employees and the local community that you care about your workers. Therefore, you think that the mission statement should include wording about the importance of the employees.

### R&D Director

The company has invested heavily in research. The results have been very good. You believe that the stakeholders should see that the company is investing for tomorrow's products. You think that the mission statement should include wording about product improvement.

### Finance Director

You have kept a tight rein on the company finances. You are proud that the company is financially sound and that there have been no scandals. You think that the mission statement should include wording about the financial security of the company.

### Production Director

You are concerned with the organization of production. This includes time and cost factors. You believe that the mission statement should mention the short lead times from development to market and the reduced production costs.

# STRATEGY MEETING 2

## Job advertisement

**ISSUE**

*Job advertising aims to find the most suitable candidate to fill a post. While the term 'recruiting' often brings to mind employment agencies and classified ads, current employees are often the largest source of recruits through newsletters and bulletin boards. External advertising includes local and national newspapers which have different readerships and are appropriate for different kinds of jobs. Finally, there are different kinds of agencies which specialize in finding suitable candidates.*

*As the personnel team, your task is:*

- *to find suitable candidates for the following posts*
- *to decide how you will recruit them*
- *to design job advertisements for the posts.*

*The posts to be filled are:*

- *an executive secretary for the Marketing Manager*
- *three production line workers*
- *a supervisor for the packaging area.*

**AGENDA**

    **1 Review the posts to be filled**

    **2 Channels of recruitment**

    **3 The wording of the advertisement**

*Notes to the agenda*

    1 The Marketing Manager will present the profile of the executive secretary.

    2 The Production Manager will present the profile of the production line workers.

    3 The Factory Manager will present the profile of the supervisor.

    4 The meeting participants will discuss the possible channels of recruitment.

    5 The participants will work in pairs to draft the advertisements or requirements for the three jobs.

# Strategy Meeting 2

## Continued . . .

## ROLES AND CONTRIBUTIONS

### *Marketing Manager*

The secretary should be well-organized, competent, and hard-working. He or she should be able to take initiatives and produce results with the minimum of supervision. He or she will need to be able to work together with others. He or she should have at least 10 years' experience and have held a similar position. Knowledge of Office Software is a must.

### *Production Manager*

The production line workers need to be hard-working and reliable. They will be trained on the job, but should have had previous experience of working on a production line. You would like to employ women, as you have found that they are better suited to the demands of the job. On the other hand, with their home commitments, they are less flexible when it comes to overtime working.

### *Factory Manager*

The supervisor will, above all, need to be able to handle people. The ideal candidate will have had at least 5 years' experience of working in a supervisory position in a manufacturing company. The job will involve shift working.

### *Personnel Manager*

You favour using the internal bulletin boards. These have always proved a useful starting point and give a quick response at a low cost. If there is no response, then you would consider other channels.

### *Employee Relations Manager*

You favour using the local newspaper. It reaches a wide readership and can be used for all non-specialist positions. In this case you believe that all the posts could be successfully filled by recruiting from the local community.

### *Recruitment and Selection Manager*

You have had a lot of experience of working with Smith and Bell, who specialize in the recruitment of executive secretaries. You believe that they should be given the task of finding suitable candidates. You believe the other posts could be filled either by using the bulletin boards or the company newsletter.

# STRATEGY MEETING 3

## Market research questionnaire

**ISSUE**

Market research aims to find about consumers' needs so that manufacturers and producers can develop and price products more appropriately. It is now common practice for market research companies to sell the results of surveys to companies.

You are members of a team responsible for market research questionnaire design. You have been asked to design a questionnaire which will be mailed to a large number of households. In order to encourage a response, your clients are making the following free offers:

- money-saving coupons for the clients' products
- cash prizes to respondents
- special offers to selected respondents.

Your clients operate in a number of different sectors. Their aim is to get information about the profile of existing and potential users of their products and services. The sectors are:

- mobile phones
- holiday travel
- fast food restaurants
- tobacco
- banking

First discuss the main categories for your questionnaire, then design a questionnaire to be sent to households.

**AGENDA**

1. Review objective of exercise
2. The main categories and sections of the questionnaire
3. The design of the questionnaire

*Notes to the agenda*

1. The Team Leader will present the objectives of the exercise and agree the results to be achieved.
2. The participants will agree on the main categories of the questionnaire and decide on the sections.
3. The participants will work in pairs to draft the questions for specific sections of the questionnaire.

# Strategy Meeting 3

*Continued . . .*

## ROLES AND CONTRIBUTIONS

### Participant 1

You are responsible for the client in the mobile phone sector. Your client will want to know about the profile of existing and potential mobile users. In addition, the client will want to know what types of services they require and what they are prepared to pay for these services.

### Participant 2

You are responsible for the client in the holiday travel sector. Your client will want to know how many holidays are taken a year, what destinations are visited and how much people are prepared to spend on their holiday, as well as during their holiday.

### Participant 3

You are responsible for the client in the fast food sector. Your client will want to know about attitudes to fast food and to fast food restaurants. In addition, they will want details of the types of fast food eaten, the frequency of visits, and the amount spent per person per visit.

### Participant 4

You are responsible for the client in the tobacco sector. Your client will want to know about attitudes to smoking. In addition, they will want details of cigarettes in terms of brands smoked and consumption. They would also like to know whether people are sufficiently warned about the risks of smoking.

### Participant 5

You are responsible for the client in the banking sector. Your client will want to know about the profile of existing and potential clients. In addition, the client will want to know what types of services they require and what they are prepared to pay for these services.

### Team Leader

You need to ensure that the questionnaire covers the main sections above. In addition, it should include some general information about the household, including number of people, age group, professional status and income bracket.

# STRATEGY MEETING 4

## Early retirement document

**ISSUE**

*ITCorp is being taken over by MegaCorp. As a result of the acquisition, it is expected that some of ITCorp's supervisory and middle managers will need to go. In order to avoid making some 50 members of staff redundant, it is proposed to offer them an early retirement package. The financial terms are reasonably attractive and it is expected that most of them will take up the offer.*

*Your task is to draft a letter to highlight the opportunities that early retirement offers.*

*First discuss the opportunities that early retirement offers, then write the document to be sent to designated 50 members of staff.*

**AGENDA**

1. Review objective of exercise
2. The opportunities of early retirement
3. Drafting the letter

*Notes to the agenda*

1. The Team Leader will present the objectives of the exercise and agree on the working procedures.
2. The participants will discuss the opportunities of early retirement in order to produce a check-list of points to be covered in the letter.
3. The participants will work on a draft of the early retirement letter.

# Strategy Meeting 4

*Continued . . .*

## ROLES AND CONTRIBUTIONS

### Participant 1

You believe that the opportunities for leisure activities will be attractive to the retirers. Their secure financial position will enable them to pursue, within reason, a range of different activities. You think the letter should outline the attractive possibilities.

### Participant 2

This is a unique opportunity for further personal development. You know that some of the managers would like to extend their interests. Their work in the company has kept them very busy during the acquisition. Now is the ideal moment for them to expand their horizons. You think the letter should outline the attractive possibilities.

### Participant 3

There is a working life after early retirement. As some of the managers are still quite young, they should feel that they can still contribute to the business environment. You feel that they should realize the potential for using their knowledge and expertise in new areas. Consultancy offers many opportunities. You think the letter should outline the attractive possibilities.

### Participant 4

You believe that the main attraction of early retirement is that the managers can now enjoy a flexible lifestyle. No longer tied to the 'corporate treadmill', they will be able to make their own decisions about how they want to spend their days. You think the letter should outline the attractive possibilities of a more flexible lifestyle.

### Participant 5

The early retirement financial package will provide security for the managers. In these uncertain times, you feel that the letter should emphasize this point and outline the attractive possibilities.

### Team Leader

You need to ensure that the letter covers the relevant main points, including the reasons for reducing the management headcount. In addition, it should be written in an appropriate tone, which values the past contributions and emphasizes the positive aspects of early retirement.

# BRAINSTORMING 1

## Managing your time

Effective time management is a key concern for every manager. With growing pressure on managers to complete more and more tasks, time is becoming an extremely precious commodity – to be saved and spent carefully. While many managers now have electronic agendas to keep their appointments in order, there are still many ways in which they could improve their time management skills.

You have been set up as a project team to investigate the effective use of management time. Your tasks are to:

- identify the main causes of time-wasting among managers
- suggest steps to reduce the time-wasting
- design a reminder for managers about the importance of the effective use of time.

# BRAINSTORMING 2

## Management tools

---

*In its broadest sense, management is the skill which enables companies to thrive. In some senses, management follows trends in fashion. Early models of management were concerned with maximizing output by measuring the precise requirements of the job. Subsequent theories of management have recognized the human element and added motivation as one of the keys to successful management.*

*In addition to management theories, there have been management tools which have helped managers achieve their objectives. These have included:*

- *effective team-building*
- *effective project management*
- *effective delegation*
- *effective time management.*

*Your task is to devise a new set of management tools. Your starting point should be to identify an area in which managers need help or assistance. Your next step is to create a tool which will help managers perform this task more efficiently.*

# BRAINSTORMING 3

## What's in a name?

Your company manufactures bicycles. It is about to launch a new adult bike: a cross between a mountain bike and a tourer (a so-called hybrid). The bike will be priced for the top end of the market and hopes to attract buyers in the AB social economic class.

As with all such products, the name is crucial. It needs to be a name which can be used across the world as you hope to sell it into both the domestic and export markets.

The agenda below is designed to support the brainstorming process.

**AGENDA**

1. Presentation of the product
2. Presentation of a typical customer
3. Brainstorming on the name
4. Decision

*Notes to the agenda*

1. *Presentation of the product*
   The Product Manager will present the new bike.
2. *Presentation of a typical customer*
   The Marketing Manager will talk about the target customer.
3. *Brainstorming on the name*
   The meeting will brainstorm the name.
4. *Decision*
   A decision will be made.

# Brainstorming 3

## Continued . . .

**ROLES**

*Product Manager*

Your task is to present the bike. If possible find a picture of a bike.

*Main features:*
    lightweight alloy frame
    twist-operated gear change
    six gears
    comfortable seat and sitting position
    solid but attractive design
    dark green frame

*Marketing Manager*

Your main task is to present the target customer:

Age: 30–50
Sex: male
Married with young children
Lives in detached house
Annual Income: £25,000 plus
Sport-oriented
Will use bike at weekends with family, mainly on local trips

**Note**: Expand on the description as you like.

*Other roles (4/5 participants)*

Your main task is to brainstorm the name.

# BRAINSTORMING 4

## A new logo

---

You own an information technology (IT) consultancy company called 'Computer Solutions'. You started the company 10 years ago offering IT support to local companies: advising about hardware and software and also maintaining customer systems. Your company has expanded considerably over the last five years and now operates throughout the continent. Its image remains rather domestic and even provincial:

You have decided to give the company a stronger brand image by changing the logo.

To start the process you have collected together some design ideas. Discuss these ideas.

# Brainstorming 4

## Continued . . .

**ROLES**

You are all partners/owners of the company called 'Computer Solutions'. Some initial positions are outlined below.

*Partner 1*

You think the logo should be in simple colours and based around the letters C and S.

*Partner 2*

You think the global nature of the business should be emphasized with a globe as part of the logo.

*Partner 3*

You think the activity itself (computer support) should be visualized in the logo.

*Partner 4*

You think the concept of a solution should be visualized in some way.

*Partner 5*

You like the existing logo. You can't understand why you need to change it.

*Partner 6*

You think the new logo must look similar to the existing logo, otherwise customers will not identify with it.

*Partner 7*

You think the new logo must look dynamic – some movement in the design is important.

*Partner 8*

You think the name 'Computer Solutions' is more important than the logo design.

# BRAINSTORMING 5

## The company excursion

*Every year your company takes all the employees (125 people) on an excursion. The trip usually consists of some kind of entertainment in the evening, plus lunch and maybe a tour during the day. The objective is to do something all together.*

*Your task is to brainstorm what kind of trip should be organized for this year. Some alternatives are listed below:*

A castle

A public garden

A leisure complex

A funfair

A walk in the country

A city tour

A city show/play

Dinner in a city restaurant

Dinner in a country restaurant

Spectating at a sports event (grand prix, tennis tournament)

Participating in a sports event (horse riding, archery, etc.)

Outdoor pursuit (orienteering, rock climbing, canoeing, white water rafting)

Open-roof bus tour

Other ideas . . .

# Language functions for meetings

## LANGUAGE FOR CHAIRING A MEETING

### Opening the meeting
Good morning/afternoon, everyone.
If we are all here, let's . . .
. . . get started
. . . start the meeting.
. . . start.

### Welcoming and introducing participants
We're pleased to welcome . . .
It's a pleasure to welcome . . .
I'd like to introduce . . .
I don't think you've met . . .

### Stating the purpose/objective/aim
We're here today to . . .
Our aim is to . . .
I've called this meeting in order to . . .
By the end of this meeting, we need a clear recommendation.

### Giving apologies for absence
I'm afraid . . . can't be with us today. She is in . . .
I have received apologies for absence from . . ., who is in . . .

### Reading the secretary's report of last meeting
First let's go over the report from the last meeting, which was held on . . .
Here are the minutes from our last meeting, which was on . . .

### Dealing with Matters Arising
Peter, how is the information technology (IT) project progressing?
Sarah, have you completed the report on the new accounting package?
Has everyone received a copy of Jeremy's report on his marketing visit?
So, if there are no other matters arising, let's move on to today's agenda.

### Introducing the agenda
Have you all seen a copy of the agenda?
There are three items on the agenda. First, . . ., second, . . . and third, . . .
Shall we take the points in this order?
I suggest we take item 2 last.
Is there Any Other Business?

### Allocating roles (secretary, participants and chairperson)
. . . has agreed to take the minutes.
. . ., would you mind taking the minutes?
. . . has kindly agreed to give us a report on this matter.
. . . will lead point 1, . . . point 2, and . . . point 3.

**Agreeing the ground rules for the meeting (contributions, timing, decision-making, etc)**
We will hear a short report on each point first, followed by a discussion round the table.
I suggest we go round the table first.
The meeting is due to finish at . . .
We'll have to keep each item to ten minutes. Otherwise we'll never get through.
We may need to vote on item 5, if we can't get a unanimous decision.

**Introducing the first item**
So, let's start with . . .
Shall we start with . . .?
So, the first item on the agenda is . . .
Pete, would you like to kick off?
Martin, would you like to introduce this item?

**Closing an item**
I think that covers the first item.
Shall we leave that item?
If nobody has anything else to add, . . .

**Next item**
. . . let's move onto the next item
The next item on the agenda is . . .
Now we come to the question of . . .

**Asking for contributions**
We haven't heard from you yet, George. What do you think about this proposal?
Would you like to add anything, Anne?
Anything to add, Helen?

**Handing over to another person**
I'd like to hand over to Mark, who is going to lead the next point.
Right, Dorothy, over to you.

**Keeping the meeting on target (time, relevance, decisions)**
We're running short of time.
Please be brief.
I'm afraid we've run out of time.
We'll have to leave that to another time.
I'm afraid that's outside the scope of this meeting.
We're beginning to lose sight of the main point.
Keep to the point, please.
I think we'd better leave that for another meeting.
Are we ready to make a decision?
Shall we vote on Mary's proposal?

**Clarifying**
Let me spell out . . .
Is that clear?
Do you all see what I'm getting at?

to clarify
to explain
to interpret
to put another way
to put in other words
to recap

### Summarizing
Before we close, let me just summarize the main points.
To sum up, . . .
In brief, . . .
Shall I go over the main points?

a summary
a report
a write-up

### Agenda completed
Right, it looks as though we've covered the main items.
Is there Any Other Business?

### Agreeing time, date and place for next meeting
Can we fix the next meeting, please?
So, the next meeting will be on . . . (day), the . . . (date) of . . . (month) at . . . (time) in the meeting room. Is that OK for everyone?
What about the following Wednesday? How is that?
So, see you all then.

### Thanking participants for attending
I'd like to thank Marianne and Jeremy for coming over from London.
Thank you all for attending.
Thanks for your participation.

### Closing meeting
The meeting is closed.
I declare the meeting closed.

## LANGUAGE FOR PARTICIPATING IN A MEETING

**Getting the chairperson's attention**
(Mister/Madam) chairman.
Excuse me for interrupting.
May I come in here?

**Giving and seeking opinions**
I'm sure/convinced/positive that . . .
I (really) feel that . . .
In my opinion . . .
I tend to think that . . .
Are you sure/convinced/positive that . . .
Do you (really) think that . . .?
Am I right in thinking that . . .

**Commenting**
That's interesting . . .
Good point!
I see what you mean.

**Agreeing and disagreeing**
I totally agree with you.
Up to a point I agree with you, but . . .
(I'm afraid) I can't agree

**Advising and suggesting**
Let's . . .
We should . . ..
Why don't you . . ..
How about . . ..
I suggest/recommend that . . ..

**Requesting information and action**
Please, could you . . .
I'd like you to . . .
I wonder if you could . . .

## DEALING WITH COMMUNICATION PROBLEMS

### Asking for repetition
I didn't catch that. Could you repeat that, please?
Sorry, I missed that. Could you say it again, please?

### Asking for clarification
I don't quite follow you. What exactly do you mean?
I don't see what you mean. Could we have some more details, please?

### Asking for verification
You *did* say March, didn't you? ('did' is stressed)
Is it true that we'll be moving in March?

### Asking for spelling
Could you spell that, please?

### Correcting information
Sorry, I think you misunderstood what I said. The move will be in March.
Sorry, that's not quite right. We'll be here until March.

### Language for recording the meeting

### Listing the names of the participants
Present: . . . (names or initials)
Apologies for absence received from: . . . (names or initials).

### Describing the topics discussed
. . . (name) reported on/presented/considered/discussed/evaluated/proposed . . .

### Giving details of arguments for and against
. . . (name) pointed out/observed/stated that . . .
. . . (name) disagreed with/voiced reservations about/opposed/objected to . . .

### Describing the decisions made
The meeting agreed to . . .
It was (unanimously) agreed that we would . . .
. . . (item) was postponed until the next meeting on . . .

### Describing voting details
Three voted for the motion; two voted against.
The motion was carried by three votes to two.
The proposal was defeated by three votes to two.

### Describing follow-up actions to be carried out (who, what and when)
. . . (name) will prepare a report by . . . (date)
. . . (name) agreed to evaluate the new software by . . . (date)
It was agreed that . . . (name) would present the findings to the next meeting on . . . (date)

### Showing the date, time and place of the next meeting
The next meeting will be held on . . . (date) at . . . (time) in . . . (place)
Next meeting: . . . (time) on . . . (date) in . . . (place)

# Social Aspects of meetings

## THE SOCIAL ETIQUETTE OF MEETINGS

**Complete the following questionnaire and then compare it with a partner's**

1 I *enjoy/don't like** participating in small talk.

2 In my country small talk *plays/does not play* an important role.

3 Before a meeting we usually talk about:
   a) *the weather*
   b) *our families*
   c) *sport*
   d) *today's news*

4 Small talk before a meeting usually lasts:
   a) *1 minute*
   b) *5 minutes*
   c) *15 minutes*
   d) *more than 15 minutes*

5 At meetings we usually wear:
   a) *a jacket and tie*
   b) *dress/skirt and shirt/blouse*
   c) *casual clothes*

6 We *never/always/sometimes* use first names in meetings.
7 I *don't think/think* it is important to distinguish between a chairman and a chairwoman.
8 The chairman in a meeting is *usually/sometimes* the boss.
9 For me chairman means *boss/facilitator*.
10 The secretary in a meeting *is always a woman/can be a man or a woman*.
11 We arrange seating *with the chairman at the top of the table/with everybody* around the table.
12 We *always/sometimes/never* serve coffee during meetings.

* delete as appropriate

## ARE YOU A MEETING PERSON?

**Complete the following questionnaire. When you have finished, add up your score and refer to the answer key.**

*Question*                                                      *Score*

1  I like speaking                                               (3)
   I don't mind speaking in meetings                             (2)
   I don't like speaking in meetings                             (1)

2  When somebody dominates a meeting:
   I try to interrupt and shut him/her up                        (3)
   I think about other things                                    (2)
   I listen                                                      (1)

3  When I am chairing a meeting:
   I control the discussion a lot                                (3)
   I allow the participants freedom                              (2)
   I play a passive role                                         (1)

4  Before a meeting
   I never prepare                                               (3)
   I sometimes prepare                                           (2)
   I always prepare                                              (1)

5  I often find meetings:
   are too short                                                 (3)
   are usually the right length                                  (2)
   are too long                                                  (1)

6  I see most meetings as:
   An opportunity to discuss and air ideas                       (3)
   A chance to do business                                       (2)
   A necessary evil                                              (1)

*Answer key*

- 6–9: You see little value in meetings. You are an introverted type who works best on your own. You tolerate other people but don't benefit from sharing ideas with them.
- 10–14: Meetings can be useful for you. You are quite independent and don't need contact with people.
- 15–18: Meetings are an important part of your working life. You are extroverted and like to talk things through.